Columbus and
the World Around Him

ALSO BY MILTON MELTZER

African-American History
(with Langston Hughes and C. Eric Lincoln)

Ain't Gonna Study War No More:
The Story of America's Peace-Seekers

All Times, All Peoples:
A World History of Slavery

The American Revolutionaries:
A History in Their Own Words 1750–1800

Benjamin Franklin: The New American

The Black Americans:
A History in Their Own Words

Crime in America

Dorothea Lange:
Life Through the Camera

The Jewish Americans:
A History in Their Own Words

Langston Hughes: A Biography

Mark Twain:
A Writer's Life

Mary McLeod Bethune:
Voice of Black Hope

Never to Forget:
The Jews of the Holocaust

Rescue: The Story of How Gentiles
Saved Jews During the Holocaust

Starting from Home:
A Writer's Beginnings

Voices from the Civil War

Columbus
and the
World Around Him

by Milton Meltzer

FRANKLIN WATTS
New York / London / Toronto / Sydney / 1990

Maps by Joe LeMonnier

Photographs courtesy of Bettmann Archive: pp. 11, 30 (top right
and bottom), 34, 39, 68, 73, 114, 115, 120, 121, 134, 152, 157 (top left
and bottom), 164; Bodleian Library, Oxford: p. 14; New York Public
Library Picture Collection: pp. 17, 23, 30 (top left), 43, 46, 50, 58, 76,
79, 92, 95 (all), 100, 104, 126, 143 (both), 157 (top right), 177 (both),
179; Culver Pictures: pp. 21, 33; National Maritime Museum, London:
p. 53; Art Resource: p. 62; U.S. Capitol Historical Society: p. 85;
Museum of the American Indian, Heye Foundation: p. 165; James
Ford Bell Library, University of Minnesota: p. 173.

Library of Congress Cataloging-in-Publication Data

Meltzer, Milton, 1915–

Columbus and the world around him / Milton Meltzer.
p. cm.
Includes bibliographical references.
Summary: Describes the voyages of Columbus, the terrible impact of
the Spaniards on the Indians, and the ultimate cultural influence of
the Native Americans on their white conquerors.
ISBN 0-531-15148-4 — 0-531-10899-6 (lib. bdg.)
1. Columbus, Christopher—Juvenile literature. 2. Explorers—
Spain—Biography—Juvenile literature. 3. Explorers—America—
Biography—Juvenile literature. 4. America—Discovery and
exploration—Spanish—Juvenile literature. [1. Columbus,
Christopher. 2. Explorers. 3. America—Discovery and exploration—
Spanish.] I. Title.
E111.M49 1990
970.01'5—dc20
[B] [92] 89-24764 CIP AC

Contents

Columbus and
the World Around Him

1

Only Three Continents

When the historians tell us that Columbus "discovered" America, what do they mean?

Surely not that no one knew America was there.

It was there all right, and millions of people were living in it. Their ancestors, the first immigrants, had probably arrived on foot about 25,000 years before, over a land bridge that then traversed the region between present-day Siberia and Alaska. They walked thousands of miles, over thousands of years, spreading all the way to the tip of South America. These Native Americans knew where *they* were.

It was Columbus who didn't know where he was. When he reached America in 1492, he discovered what had existed before but had remained unknown to him, and to the people of Europe.

He wasn't looking for America when he set sail from Spain. The maps of the world he had seen showed no such continent. The map makers knew only of Europe, Asia, and Africa. When they tried to represent the planet on their sheets, they depicted the three continents as a huge blob of earth with some seas cutting into it.

To the Europeans, the Mediterranean Sea was the center of the world, with Europe above it, Africa below it, and the edge of Asia bordering its eastern rim. The Europeans knew something about the lands of North Africa and the Middle East, and little more. The rest was guesswork, legend, mystery.

What they never knew, or what had been forgotten, was that long before Columbus, other European seafarers, the Norse, had leapfrogged Atlantic islands to find America. According to Norse sagas, around the year 870, their seafarers had settled in Iceland, an island in the North Atlantic some 800 miles (1,300 km) west of Norway. The Norseman Eric the Red moved his family there a hundred years later. Then in 985 he discovered Greenland, a much bigger island west of Iceland, and founded a settlement.

One day a shipload of Icelanders heading for Greenland was driven off course by a great storm. As the weather lifted, they saw a strange coast, thickly wooded, but did not venture ashore. When they finally reached Greenland, their tale of "a land covered with trees" was exciting news to people struggling to make a living on bare rocky soil.

Leif Ericsson, the son of Eric the Red, decided to find and explore that new land. When he came upon it, he called the place Vinland because its wild berries looked like grapes. Leif's company stayed only a few months, but soon a friend of his sailed to Vinland with three boats and 160 people to start a settlement on what promised to be better farmland than they had known. These first immigrants, according to the saga, stayed in Vinland for about three years. But when they were attacked by some Native Americans (perhaps Eskimos) they fled back to Greenland.

Were these stories rooted in fact, or were they fantasy? Archeologists looked long for the remnants of such a settlement, but not until the 1960s did they uncover the foundations of rough Norse houses in Newfoundland, and some debatable evidence of settlement on the New England coast. The scholars who doubted the landings of the Norse seafarers had ever happened were convinced now of their reality.

Type of vessel used in Norse voyages to
North America in 9th and 10th centuries

Why did that first settlement of Europeans in America not endure? The winters were too harsh, the settlers too few, the natives too dangerous. The resources needed for a persistent effort to bridge the Atlantic simply did not exist in the tenth century. It took hundreds of years for medieval Europe to reach the stage where the voyage of Columbus would have its explosive effect upon the Americas, and upon Europe.

While the Norse were finding their way to America, the Europeans began to learn more about a larger world. It was the Crusades that opened the way. These religious wars began in 1096 and did not end until 200 years later. Hordes of nobles, knights, monks, and peasants set off from Christian Europe to free the Holy Land from the Moslem infidels. Each of the four Crusades failed as military operations, but their commercial effects were great. The Crusaders returning to Europe told of great cities, busy markets, and the pleasures of such luxuries as spices, silks, and jewels.

As Europeans began to demand these goods, merchants in the Italian seaport cities set up trade arrangements with the powerful Moslem rulers. The Italians monopolized the highly profitable business carried along trading routes between Europe and the Asian lands to the east. Out of Asia's treasure-houses came tea, spices, and pepper for the tables of the rich, silks and gold brocades for their dresses and draperies, precious jewels for their rings and bracelets. To pay for these imports, the Italians exported woolen and linen textiles, arms and armor, copper, lead, tin, coral, bullion, and Caucasian slaves. The goods they received in exchange they sold at high prices to other Europeans. Venice and Genoa were the main centers for distributing Eastern luxury goods to western and northern Europe. The products were moved by river, by pack train, and by sea.

To bypass the Italian grip on eastern trade, other European powers began to look for other sources of supply, or for other routes to the same sources.

The Europeans knew little about the great continent of Asia. Their information came from travelers' stories, hearsay, myth, and the speculations of scholars. Direct, hard facts were scanty. The Romans, in the heyday of their power, had imported spices from India and silk from China. As their empire crumbled, so did their contacts with the Orient. And the conquests of the Moslemized Arabs that began in the seventh century cut Europe off from penetrating Asia any further than Syria, Palestine, and Egypt.

Until the Italian Marco Polo's great travel book appeared in the early fourteenth century, there was no European account of India or China worth much. As a young man Polo had traveled to Asia, spending twenty years in China in the court of its great ruler, Kublai Khan. Polo's book roused the curiosity of adventurers, merchants, and rulers.

The report of other merchants and missionaries added something to the limited state of knowledge about Asia. But Marco Polo's *Description of the World* was the best of all accounts of Asia to come from medieval travelers. His book also added to knowledge of the seas. On his outbound journey he had sailed the Mediterranean from Venice to Alexandretta, and gone the rest of the way by land. On his homeward journey, however, he went partly by water, ticking off ports in Indochina, Sumatra, Ceylon, western India, and the Persian Gulf. He was the first European to report on the Malay archipelago, and that east of China lay "Cipango"—Japan—a rich island kingdom he had never seen but had heard described.

But to reach Marco Polo's dreamlike Orient you needed unbounded time and unlimited courage. To travel overland from Italy to China could take a year. And could you be sure of reaching that market? Thieves lay everywhere in wait, avalanches off the high mountains could bury your company alive, burning desert heats could drive you mad. And if you did arrive in the heart of Asia, could you bring back your treasure safely? The same dangers threatened your returning caravan.

An illuminated manuscript depicts
Marco Polo's departure from Venice
on his journey to China in 1271.

If only you could reach the Orient by sea! That would make an enormous difference. No thieves to fear, no mountains to climb, no deserts to cross. And no donkeys, horses, or camels needed to pack your treasures home: just the capacious hold of your own ship.

It became clear that the more profitable—and dependable—way to tap the remote market sources would be by sea. Yet there seemed no way to reach the Orient by water. Yes, Marco Polo had sailed some of his way home. But much of his journey was made by land. Could you reach Asia by sailing *west* from Europe?

In theory, perhaps. In the 1400s educated people commonly believed that the earth was round. They acquired that knowledge from the thinkers of ancient times. The Greek world had produced a school of geographers and mathematicians. One of them, Eratosthenes, had figured out the circumference of the earth and reached a surprisingly true answer. He and Strabo, a geographer, described fairly well the continents they knew something about. Where they were ignorant, they left a blank and assumed a vast ocean surrounded the continents. The man who went furthest in geographical study was the Egyptian Ptolemy. Around 130 A.D. he wrote two major works, one on astronomy and the other on geography.

Long after the ancients came the Arab scholars. Their cosmographers tried to shape a general picture of the world based on Ptolemy's description. The Arabs, however, had little to add through actual exploration, for their journeys by land and sea were limited to the Mediterranean and the region bordering the north Indian Ocean, and these areas were already known to the ancient Greeks. The Atlantic, the Arabs said, could not be navigated; it was "the green sea of darkness." Their dread of the vast unknown sea was picked up by the medieval Europeans, and passed along by the academic geographers who mixed Ptolemy's work with Arab theories.

Reading the European books of that time, you find them filled with references to the Bible, with legends, and with traveler's tales. They are likely to quote the Greek, Latin, and Arab authorities, but they are far from the real world of ships and sailing. One of the books, *Imago Mundi* by Pierre Cardinal d'Ailly, is among the few Columbus studied. It appeared in 1410, the same year Ptolemy's *Geography* was published in Latin translation. The recovery from long obscurity of that ancient text spurred the development of scientific geography.

While Ptolemy's map of the world pictured fairly well the Roman Empire of his day, it contained many errors. What Ptolemy didn't know, he imagined. Not content to leave blank spaces, he filled them in with his dreams. He made up a huge southern continent tied to Africa at one end and to China at the other. The Indian Ocean he pictured as an inland sea, a closed sea, its southern shore touching the unknown southern continent. From his map it appeared you could not reach the Indies (by which was meant the East Indies, China, and the Malay peninsula) by sea. That door to the treasure-house was shut. (Strabo, however, who wrote before Ptolemy, believed that Africa *could* be circumnavigated.) The whole southern hemisphere, Ptolemy said, couldn't be traveled because it was intolerably hot. And for Eratosthenes's estimate of the globe's circumference, he substituted his own guess, which was below the real measure by at least one-sixth. For some 200 years Ptolemy's *Geography* held sway over medieval geographers, though

Ptolemy's map of the world, in the Ulm edition of 1482. With a magnifying glass, see how may errors you can find in his placement of the regions of the earth.

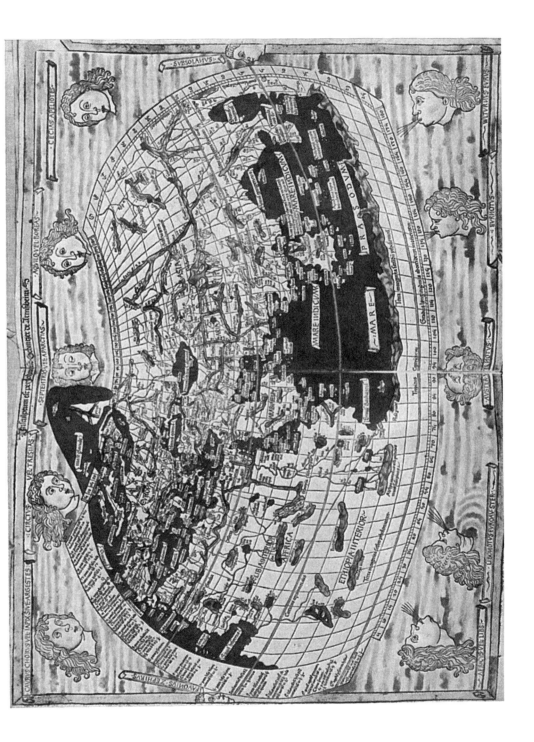

some disputed it. It would take practical voyages to prove how and where he was wrong.

What, then, was a venturesome sailor to think? If he knew anything about the writings of the academic geographers—and that was not too likely—it was discouraging. As for the maps of the world they published, he could make little use of them as guides to oceangoing voyages.

Seamen in that time, unlike those today, were almost a people apart. They were both practical and conservative, relying on traditional skills and the long experience of the past. They knew the trade routes of the Mediterranean, the Black Sea, and the coasts of western Europe. The charts and sailing directions they had developed were steady guides to their voyages. Their instruments—compass and lead line, straightedge and dividers—were accurate enough to draw and follow courses on their charts. But it was only for the regular trade routes that these instruments and their experience were useful. What was the world like beyond these regions? How could you find your way on long ocean voyages into the unknown? The answers lay only in books. And even if a sailor looked into such a book, he found guesswork and fantasy when it came to the world of the unfamiliar.

Nor did most sailors wish to try routes different from the ones they were used to. They got their living from the old trade routes; what advantage was there in venturing into the strange? Discovery for its own sake did not attract them. Their main interest in going to sea was economic. So too would be the concern of the great discoverers soon to come, and of the princes who backed their voyages.

2

To Serve God
and Grow Rich

The first great voyages of discovery were carried out mostly by the adventurous Portuguese and Spaniards, and first among them was Prince Henry of Portugal. He was later called the "Navigator," not because he went to sea himself (royalty didn't do that) but because he encouraged exploration. He furnished the ships, the money, the organization needed for the long voyages. At the age of twenty-one Henry had fought bravely in the campaign to take Ceuta, the town on the north African rim of the Mediterranean. It was the first permanent European conquest in Africa, and the Portuguese hoped it would be the gateway to new sources of gold and spices.

To pile up wealth: that was one of the two universal motives for overseas ventures. The other was to convert the pagans to Christianity, the same motive that fired the Crusades. One of the conquistadors, Bernal Diaz, put it plainly when he wrote that all his kind sailed out "to serve God and His Majesty, to give light to those who were in darkness, and to grow rich, as all men desire to do."

Ownership of land was the main way to wealth in those days. (It still is in many places.) Kings, knights, and nobles went to war to seize land from one another. But they could also get rich by finding and grabbing new land, land no one lived on or land held by people they felt to be of no consequence, no-bodies they could kill or force out.

Another method of getting rich was to engage in trade, to buy as cheaply as possible and sell as dearly as possible. As we have seen, most of the products traded to Europe came from the East or the Mediterranean and the bulk of that trade was handled by merchants of the Italian ports.

The peoples of the Atlantic coast envied the Mediterranean trade and were eager to grab their share. Portuguese shippers did well dealing in wine, fish, and salt, but they saw fatter profits in gold, spices, and sugar. Yet it would be hard to slice away some of the Italians' business, protected as it was by strong naval forces and old ties with the East. So when the Portuguese made a beginning by sailing to West Africa and capturing Ceuta, it showed such ventures for new lands and new trading centers were not as difficult or risky as feared.

Prince Henry's success at Ceuta inspired him. He wanted to expand his knowledge of Africa, and in 1416 he founded in Portugal a naval arsenal at Sagres on Cape Vincent. It would serve as a base for exploration. The Atlantic was Portugal's waterway, but except for its coastline her sailors knew little about it. The huge ocean runs north and south from the Arctic to the sub-Antarctic. It stretches east and west between the continents of Europe and Africa to the then unknown continents of North and South America. What Henry's seafarers began to do was inch their way southward, down the eastern coastline of Africa, until many decades later they would come up to the end and find a way around Africa.

In the North Atlantic, on its eastern side, there are many groups of islands. The British Isles, of course, and the Norse islands close to the Arctic Circle, whose discovery came much earlier than Henry's day. Apart from these two groups there are four main others. The Canaries, a mountainous group inhabited by a primitive people, had been known for centuries. (On Ptolemy's ancient map they were marked as the western edge of

Prince Henry the Navigator, portrayed before the African city of Ceuta, which his Portuguese troops captured in 1415

the habitable world.) Throughout the 1400s Portugal and Castile contended for their ownership. The Cape Verde Islands were still not known. The uninhabited Madeira Islands had been sighted but not yet settled. And the fertile Azores, about a third of the way across the Atlantic, would be discovered one by one by the Portuguese beginning around 1427.

Pushing ahead with his expeditions to enlarge the bounds of the known world, Henry sent ships further and further south along the West African coast. When the men came back home they spread the news that tropic seas were navigable, and told tales of black people who lived near the equator.

Henry's headquarters on Cape St. Vincent, the southwestern tip of Portugal and Europe, developed into a center for oceanic knowledge. The prince gathered all the charts and sailing directions his scouts could find and welcomed mathematicians, geographers, cartographers, astronomers, and instrument makers who might help his crews find their way to new lands across unknown seas.

A prime goal for the prince was to go beyond what we now call Cape Bojador. It sits on the western bulge of Africa, and for many years his ships failed to get beyond it. The seamen were frightened by fantasies about the terrors of the ocean south of it, and came back to Henry time and again with excuses for stopping at the Cape. Finally his captain Gil Eannes rounded the Cape in 1434 and found the sea south of it was much like the sea north of it. The fearful myth of that "green sea of darkness" was fading. Soon the Portuguese established a trading fort on the African coast and were dealing in slaves and gold. It was the first European trading factory overseas. Dozens of Henry's ships sailed regularly for the Guinea coast. His men penetrated into the Sudan and discovered the Senegal River.

As exploration proved its commercial value, Henry's king gave him the monopoly of travel and trade on the Guinea coast. The pope strengthened the claim to sole rights by conferring on Henry the monopoly of converting the African blacks to Chris-

*Types of caravels, drawn for a book
on navigation in 1545*

tianity. It began the practice of calling upon the Vatican for the stamp of approval on overseas discoveries.

Prince Henry did not back his costly program of exploration out of scientific curiosity. His purpose was practical. He wanted to find the countries from which the gold came that reached north Africa by desert routes. He meant to deal directly with them and use the profits to maintain his royal household. At the same time he could serve God by making alliances with any Christian rulers his explorers might encounter below the lands of the Moslems.

And then there was his horoscope. It predicted the prince would "engage in great and noble conquests, and above all . . . attempt the discovery of things which were hidden from other men." Henry wanted badly to fulfill that horoscope. In medieval times faith in one's horoscope was common; what astronomers knew was used as much for fortune-telling as for navigation.

While Henry sent many of his ships south down the coast of Africa he directed others westward into the Atlantic. It was under his charter that Madeira was settled and turned into a prosperous trading center. From the islands came profitable timber, sugar, and the famous Madeira wine. Portugal settled the Cape Verde Islands in the 1460s. Earlier she had planted colonies in the Azores, which became the westernmost reach of Europe, the last outpost for the small fleet Columbus would command.

These Atlantic islands were important to Portugal. Crops grown on them were profitable, and control over them prevented other powers from using them to interfere with Portuguese trade in West Africa. They would make useful ports of call should anyone try to reach Asia by sailing west.

No one could guess how many other islands lay scattered in the Atlantic. Explorers hopped from one island to the next and the next, and people began to feel there was no limit. Someday would a dreaming sailor find the chain of islands off the east coast of Asia pictured in travelers' tales?

3

A New Age
Begins

It was Christopher Columbus, of course, who first spied those strange islands on the far western horizon. Only they were not off the coast of Asia, but the coast of the unknown Americas. The East Indies—Asia itself—lay thousands of miles further west.

The story of Columbus the man is astonishing in many ways. But before beginning it, let's look at the Europe he sprang from. Every one of us is the product of both our own nature—the genes we are endowed with—and the world we grow up in. Columbus was born on the dividing line between two worlds: the old one of the medieval era, or the Middle Ages, and the new one of the Renaissance, or the modern age.

The Middle Ages are placed between about 450 A.D. with the breakup of the Roman Empire, and the 1400s. Such dates are only very rough bounds; social change can never be pinpointed. The processes that make for change from the old to the new overlap in time and flow in many directions.

By 1451, the year of Columbus's birth, the slow pace of change during the Middle Ages had quickened. A few discoveries had been made early in that era, but it took centuries more for them to be widely accepted. Replacing the simple plow by the wheeled one, and the use of the horse rather than the ox to pull it, were changes introduced far back that were still not widely used toward the close of the era. Some inventions were even forgotten with the passage of time.

The application of some great discoveries has been delayed by as much as a thousand years. Delayed by what? By prejudice. The historian of science George Sarton supplies many examples. The decimal numeral system, for instance, was probably originated in India about the fifth century, but not until the fourteenth or fifteenth century was it generally accepted in Europe, and first in Italy. It's very hard to overcome the enormous resistance of old ways of thinking—even when, as with that decimal system in place of the old Roman numerals, much time and labor could be saved in making calculations.

Dogma—rigid beliefs about what's true or right—holds people back from seeing new things, new ideas. It doesn't matter that the evidence has been made plain by careful investigation and proof. We tend to fall back upon ancient authority and deny what's right in front of us. Prejudice blinds the eye and deafens the ear.

That was especially true during the Middle Ages. That world was a limited, closed system. The scholars looked at everything from a theological or legal point of view. They could not investigate a problem without reservation and without fear. They were dogmatic. The noblest minds were burdened with many superstitions.

The era of Columbus marked a break with the past. Not clear, not abrupt, but still a time of profound change. There was a passionate attempt to rediscover and relearn what the ancient Greeks and Romans had known. And that knowledge, for the next 200 years, would lead to many brilliant innovations. A French physician, writing in 1545, tried to sum it up:

The world sailed around, the largest of Earth's continents discovered, the compass invented, the printing press sowing knowledge, gunpowder revolutionizing the art of war, ancient manuscripts rescued and the restoration of scholarship, all witness to the triumph of our New Age.

He was pointing to two great areas of discovery: the exploration of the intellectual world of the ancient Greeks and Romans by scholars, and the exploration of the earth's surface by sailors. Two technical inventions helped them greatly: the printing press for the scholars, the magnetic compass for the sailors. (More on these later.)

The term "humanism" characterizes this time of change. Humanists were concerned with the classics of antiquity and with our relation to human society rather than to God. They tried to unearth long-forgotten, neglected, or unknown Greek and Latin manuscripts, to restore them to use, to edit and evaluate them. What they rediscovered of ancient learning they translated from Greek to Latin, the language widely used by educated people, and then from Latin to the common tongue of their country. Thus ordinary people, beyond the walls of the universities, were reached by the ancient learning.

The humanists who did this work saw themselves as rebels against the medieval schools whose curriculum was chiefly concerned with the works of God. While the humanists were devoted to the remote world of the ancients, strangely their discoveries helped bring to birth new ideas about man and nature.

Gradually the view of classical knowledge shifted. First there was deferential acceptance, then doubt about some things, then the rejection of what seemed wrong or useless, and finally the replacement of the outworn with the new. Of course such a process is never smooth or easy, and it takes many years.

What could the mind of Columbus feed on when he was growing up? Schooling in his day was a narrow process of vocational training. A merchant's son would quit school around age twelve to begin learning his father's business. A lower-class boy would drop out as soon as he learned the ABCs needed to enter a craftsman's guild. The luckier few expecting to enter the church, law, or medicine got a more thorough training, learning to read and write in their own language as well as in Latin. But classes were big, books and writing materials costly. The stress was on memorizing material from old textbooks, some of them written two or three hundred years earlier. Latin was the chief subject studied, and the language used in all classes. So only a few students were exposed to humanist literature. The rich, the aristocrats, hired tutors for their sons, which meant a better chance for them to have their curiosity cultivated, their imagination stirred. It was mostly boys who had schooling; there were few opportunities for girls.

Rejecting such poor training for most people, humanists wanted to reform education. They believed we could improve ourselves by thinking, and by exercising our will to change. They looked anew at how we think, and about what. To their belief that we can form our own nature, they added the desire to help others to form theirs. Most humanists hoped to create the "all-round man"—what came to be called the "Renaissance man." They wanted everyone to know about human affairs, to understand the law, to be familiar with the history of other ages. "To be ignorant of what occurred before you were born is to remain always a child. For what is the worth of human life, unless it is woven into the life of our ancestors by the cords of history?" That could have been said in 1500, but it comes from Cicero (106 B.C.–43 B.C.), the Roman orator whose essay foreshadowed the humanist ideal.

Digging into the treasury of ancient wisdom, the humanists began to shape a more enlightened age. But no one yet believed in social progress. They did not think people could improve their physical condition, that food supplies could be increased so people need no longer go hungry, that the plagues which wiped out whole populations could be eliminated, that life could be made safer and more comfortable. Instead of optimism about man's fate enlightening the popular mind, death and impending doom darkened it.

Yet in 1492, the year Columbus first voyaged to America, an Italian humanist could write, "It is undoubtedly a golden age." And it was indeed a golden age Columbus was born into. Think of the great artists and writers and scholars who lived and worked in his day. From his own country of birth, Italy: Leonardo da Vinci (born the year after Columbus), Ghiberti, Fra Angelico, Alberti, Verocchio, Ucello, Donatello, Botticelli, Perugino, Giorgione, Mantegna, Raphael, Michelangelo. . . . And from northern Europe: Bosch, Dürer, Memling, Holbein. . . . In literature there was Dante, François Villon, Aretino, Rabelais, Erasmus, Thomas More, Machiavelli, Ariosto, Heywood, Udall, Wyatt. . . .

Most of the artists were not born aristocrats. Among their fathers were a cobbler, a tanner, a muleteer, a tailor, a poulterer. Artists had to join guilds, like other tradesmen. They worked to order, and even if their talent brought them great commissions, wealth, and fame, it didn't make them gentlemen. One writer of the period, commenting on social standing, placed artists among such "laborers" as plasterers, glaziers, and thatchers.

How far did the new humanism reach? The truth is, not many Europeans were educated enough to enjoy the life of the mind. The clergy could read and write, but not all of them, especially in rural areas. Of the working poor—and they were the largest part of the population—probably less than 1 percent could read, and even fewer, write. In the towns they did better. About 60 percent in London were literate, and maybe more in Florence. But such places were very unusual. Then too, people might be able to sign their name or write a business letter, yet never read a book or get an idea from one.

Very few could handle numbers. Many who could read and write were able to do little more than add and subtract. Fractions? Only for the few. No one learned the multiplication table

*Three giants of the golden age
Columbus was born into: from
upper left, Leonardo da Vinci,
Erasmus, and Michelangelo (in
a portrait in the Sistine Chapel
reputed to be of himself)*

or used plus, minus, equals, or multiply signs. The stubborn use of Roman numerals mentioned earlier prevailed at the cost of losing much time, space, and accuracy.

Those busy in trade or diplomacy picked up a smattering of foreign languages. Superficial, however, for the preparation of grammars and dictionaries had barely begun. Clocks had been introduced in the 1300s; most people, however, measured time by sunlight and season. They divided the day less by the hours than by mealtimes. People still lived more by the rhythms of nature than by mechanical time. Parents did not record the time of a baby's birth with any regularity. Most people could only guess what their own age was. Life was measured less by years than by the stages we all go through: infancy, youth, maturity, old age. Those stages were cruelly compressed, for the average life expectancy was only thirty-five years. Malnutrition and disease took their toll quickly.

Not many children lived even to maturity. About half, and not just the poor, died in their first year. If you lived longer, poor diet, disease, and violence threatened to cut life short. Food supplies were scanty. The usual meal was bread dipped in a thin vegetable soup. To eat fresh meat more than a dozen times a year was very uncommon. Milk, butter, and cheese were too expensive. The family pig was not eaten at home but sold for much-needed cash. The landowners savagely punished poaching for game or fish. If you didn't starve to death, malnutrition was almost sure to keep you so weak you fell prey to disease.

If disease didn't get you, violence might. The frequent wars of this period organized violence on a large scale. On their way to and from battle, armies ravaged the countryside. Bandits attacked travelers and held whole villages for ransom. Violence was a poison running through the bloodstream at all levels of society. People were killed casually in quarrels, for cheating in gambling, over malicious gossip, in drinking bouts, and in urban riots.

It was, says the Renaissance scholar J. R. Hale,

> an age brutalized by a habitual exposure to and indiffer-
> ence towards cruelty. Animal combats were common
> princely entertainments. Criminals were mutilated and
> butchered in public to large and excited audiences and
> their bodies, or fragments of them, hung on gibbets out-
> side town-walls or at crossroads. At times torture was
> carried out in public, as when in 1488 the citizens of
> Bruges bayed for the spectacle to be prolonged as long
> as possible, and in another case . . . those of Mons
> "bought a brigand, at far too high a price, for the plea-
> sure of seeing him quartered, at which the people re-
> joiced more than if a new holy body had risen from the
> dead."

The individual's sense of space in the Europe of Columbus was
shaped by the fact that it was almost entirely an agricultural
land, with great tracts of uninhabited forest and marsh and scrub.
Nine out of ten lived in scattered homes or small villages. They
passed through life without ever moving out of their own birthplace. Professor Hale estimates that the average longest journey
made by most people in their lifetimes was 15 miles (24 km).

The cities, especially the bigger ones, were the breeding
ground of new ideas. The varied mix of town dwellers, the patrons of the arts, the printing presses, the marketplaces broad-
ened one's horizon and spurred the imagination. Naples was the
largest city in Europe, with 200,000 people. Venice and Milan
each had 100,000, Florence, 70,000. Paris had about 150,000.
The Iberian cities of Toledo and Seville had over 50,000, Salamanca, 100,000, and Lisbon, 40,000. Moscow had 150,000.
Below these large cities populations fell off precipitously.

A public execution

No one in Columbus's time was called a scientist. Those who studied or taught something about the physical world were called "natural philosophers." What science there was, as we view it now, came out of concern with medicine, magic, or alchemy. If you were interested in it, you had to fit it in with another career. Leonardo, one of the greatest artists of his day, was also one of the greatest scientists. He was employed by the duke of Milan as sculptor, painter, architect, and civil and military engineer. All his life he carried on simultaneously his work as artist, scientist, and engineer. Copernicus, for another, earned his living as a churchman and a doctor while he studied astronomy.

The humanists contributed something to science by publishing ancient scientific texts. But they were chiefly interested in human behavior as seen in classical literature and did not pursue the study of nature itself. The universities cared nothing for science. They did not encourage the scientific method of observation, experiment, hypothesis, further experiment. Leonardo, with no schooling, followed his own enormously varied investigations of nature wherever his mind and imagination took him. George Sarton says he took up every question at the very beginning, like a child:

With her large fleet of ships, Venice dominated the Mediterranean. This detail from a Carpaccio painting reflects the pageantry of his 15th-century city. The class of vessel shown could be used for trade in peacetime or for transport during war.

Leonardo opened his eyes and looked straight upon the world. There were no books between nature and him; he was untrammeled by learning, prejudice or convention. He just asked himself questions, made experiments and used his common sense. The world was one to him, and so was science, and so was art. But he did not lose himself in sterile contemplation, or in verbal generalities. He tried to solve patiently each little problem separately. He saw that the only fruitful way of doing that is to first state the problem as clearly as possible, then to isolate it, to make the necessary experiments and to discuss them. Experiment is always at the bottom; mathematics, that is, reason, at the end.

Although Leonardo's scientific outlook was a rare exception, men of that age gave ample evidence of curiosity and critical judgment. Common sense led them to cause-and-effect reasoning, if not to scientific experimentation. And at the level of craft and technology, trial and error produced new methods and new tools that enabled the next generation to push progress a bit further.

Ship design, for example, was improved: by the early 1400s, vessels were sturdy enough to make the crossing of great seas possible. Navigational instruments and the astronomical tables essential to their accurate use were refined. Theories of geography and ways of imagining the spaces of earth had developed so entrancingly that adventurers knocked at the doors of princes, seeking their patronage for voyages of exploration.

4

Going to Sea

It should be easy to say when and where Columbus was born. It isn't, for no absolute proof exists of these simple facts. Disputes about his birth have filled the pages of many books. Vague too are other details of his personal history. Why should he have left confusing evidence about his identity, even to keeping facts from his own sons?

Scholars suggest one or two reasons for secrecy. One is political. If Columbus in his younger years served a country at war with Spain, then even if he were born Spanish it would have done him no good in trying to enlist royal backing for his enterprise. The second reason is religious. Some reputable researchers of our century, such as Salvador de Madariaga and Simon Wiesenthal, have dug up evidence that points to a Jewish background. There is no question, however, that he was a devout Christian. That is clear from his log and other material. But if he was a convert to Christianity, or descended from converts, it's not very likely that he would have revealed that in the Spain of the Inquisition.

Most modern authoritative sources, however, agree—on the basis of some notarial records and municipal documents—that he was born in the Italian port city of Genoa in the year 1451. That he came from an obscure family, they argue, accounts for his cloudy origins. It is enough for our purpose to know that documents testify to a young Christopher of Genoa—a maritime republic—growing up in the family headed by Domenico Columbus. Then too, historians of his own time, some of whom knew him, refer to him as Genoese. Columbus himself, however, in his own writings, mentions only once that he was Genoese. It is in a letter he wrote in 1502, while in Seville, addressed to friends in a bank at Genoa. He says, "In the city of Genoa I have my roots, and there I was born. . . . Though my body be here, my heart is forever there."

The father of Christopher was a woolen weaver, and so was *his* father, Giovanni. The Columbus family had moved recently from mountain country to try their luck in a village just outside Genoa. Giovanni took up the weaving of wool, a trade requiring moderate skill. He apprenticed his son Domenico to a Flemish weaver in the town. For five years of unpaid work, the apprentice drew board, room, and clothing. At twenty-two, Domenico settled in a neighborhood of Genoa where many wool weavers lived. By the 1440s he was a master weaver renting a house just inside the eastern gate of Genoa. His wife, Susanna, was also the child of a weaver and grew up in a mountain village. Their son was born in 1451 and they named him for St. Christopher, a legendary figure said to have lived in Asia Minor in the third century. The legend holds that he was a pagan, a giant of a man, who went out into the world looking for the Christ he had heard about. He lived in a hut on the bank of a turbulent river. There was no bridge to take travelers across safely. Christopher, using a tree trunk as his staff, would wade through the river carrying people on his powerful back.

Asleep one night, Christopher was wakened by a little child's voice calling for help to take him over the river. As Christopher struggled through the swift water the child's weight became almost unbearably heavy, and it took all the giant's strength to make it to the other side. When he put the boy down, he groaned that the whole world could hardly have weighed so much. Do

*An early woodcut of St. Christopher carrying
the infant Jesus across the river*

not marvel, the child replied, for you did bear upon your back the whole world and Him who created it. The child was Jesus, who holds the whole world in His hands.

To prove his words, He told Christopher to plant his staff near his hut and the next day it would bear him fruit. This he did, and woke in the morning to find a date palm blossoming. Christopher—the name means Christ-bearer—became the patron saint of travelers. We can imagine how the story might have charmed the boy who would become the most renowned traveler in history, believing it his mission to carry Christ's word to the unconverted.

Christopher Columbus had three brothers and a sister. His mother's life is almost a blank page. Domenico, the father, was master of his own shop, buying the wool for his looms and selling the finished cloth. He took in apprentices to teach them the trade and joined the local weavers guild, a craft that had its own chapel in the cathedral. The records suggest that Domenico had business troubles. He failed to fill orders, to pay for goods he bought, and even to furnish the dowry promised when his daughter married. Once he spent a few days in jail for not paying a debt in time. Sometimes he tried to make ends meet by selling cheeses and wines on the side. But it was not all his fault. When bad times came, Genoa's working people would be hurt most. Wool sales fell off, prices dropped, and Domenico's trade shrank.

When Christopher was eight he saw blood in the streets. A struggle for control of the city broke out between two powerful families, and men with swords chased each other through the public squares. Children were not protected from seeing such disasters. Who thought of childhood as a special, precious state? Parents dressed their children like themselves and moved them speedily into adult occupations. There were no "how to raise your child" manuals and no nurseries. No one hid the storms and griefs of life from children.

The boy must have spent much time at the harbor. It was far more exciting than the wool, the looms, the dust, and the dark of his father's workshop. Dozens of ships docked in the port, loading cargoes for the East and unloading the exotic goods brought back from their long voyages. For a time there were terrifying raids by pirates from Spain's Catalonian coast. They stormed ashore to sack the city and then sailed off with their holds full of treasure.

Hanging about the port a boy could see all kinds of people from faraway places—the Aegean islands, the Middle East, northern Europe, and North Africa. It was his first taste of the unknown. But he had to work, too. He probably helped his father, carding the wool Domenico bought, handing it to his mother to spin into yarn, and then dyeing it to make it ready for the loom. It's likely that the whole family shared in the work of weaving.

Schooling? There is no record of any for him. As we saw earlier, few people of his day got any kind of formal education. He may have picked up some scraps of learning from the friars nearby. His son Ferdinand claimed that Columbus studied at the University of Pavia, but its records disprove that. He used the common Genoese tongue—a spoken dialect, not a written language—which people from other parts of Italy could not understand. As a poor boy he never learned classical Italian, a written language. He was probably close to being illiterate, until as an adult he learned to read and write Castilian, the language of educated people on the Iberian peninsula. Earlier, living for a decade in Lisbon, he learned to speak Portuguese. Somehow he learned to use Latin too.

What the young Columbus looked like in his youth we do not know. There is no true portrait of him in existence. He seems never to have been painted or drawn from life. However, some who knew him have described his appearance. He was said to be a tall man, with a ruddy skin, red hair, and an aquiline nose. As a boy he was probably a gangling, freckled carrottop with the blue eyes that often go with that coloration.

Living in a port city gave the youngster many chances to go to sea. Later in life he said he began his seafaring at the age of ten. It couldn't have been much more than short fishing trips or maybe the brief crossing to Corsica. Perhaps he went along with merchants carrying Domenico's woolens to trade at other ports along the coast. Such voyages would have been made in small boats with the shoreline always in view. It was slow going, and would have kept him away for a few days and nights at most.

We don't know it for a fact, but it would seem likely for his father to object to his son's going to sea. Why not master the weaving trade and carry it on for the family? Besides, out at sea the boy was beyond his father's control. They may have drawn apart after some bitter quarrels, for later, in the son's time of glory, there is no evidence that he ever got in touch with his father. Nor did Columbus ever send his father any money during the years when fame and fortune came his way.

In 1470, when Columbus was nineteen, his father moved the family and his looms to Savona, a smaller coastal port just west of Genoa. There are few traces of the family in local records over the next years. Then Susanna died, and Domenico moved back to Genoa. He died some time in the 1490s, after his son's voyage to the New World.

The first chance Christopher had to sail far from home came when he was about twenty. A Genoese family of ship builders and traders sent him as a business agent on a voyage to the island of Chios, off the coast of Asia Minor. The ship, named *Roxana,* was a tall three-master, much bigger than anything he had sailed on before. It did not edge its way along the coastline but moved boldly out to the open sea.

Christopher watched how the helmsman navigated by the art of deduced, or dead, reckoning. It is a method of keeping track of a ship's course long in use. It would be used by Columbus

Genoa, the birthplace of Columbus,
in a detail from a drawing of 1485

in his voyage to the New World, and it is still practiced today by some yachtsmen. As Robert Fuson describes it:

> In dead reckoning the mariner keeps careful account of his direction by compass, speed through the water, direction and strength of winds, and perhaps leeway, the downwind skid caused by wind pressure on the hull and rigging. By plotting the direction and distance traveled by his ship, the sailor marks down what he believes is his daily position. The difficulty is that once out of sight of land, no mariner without modern aids can know what currents affect his vessel, whether they push him on his way, hinder him, or cause him to crab to the left or the right.

Home again, Columbus joined a fleet of ships bound in the opposite direction from Chios. With constant warfare and piratical raids making this end of the Mediterranean a risky route, Genoa sent a convoy of five armed merchant ships to market a cargo in northern Europe. With Columbus aboard as a common seaman, the fleet sailed in 1476, passing Gibraltar, the gateway to the Atlantic. But then a larger fleet of pirate ships attacked them in the waters off Cape St. Vincent, where Prince Henry the Navigator had made his headquarters. They grappled and fought all day, until fires and cannon sank three of the Genoese and four of the enemy ships. Hundreds of men died of the flames or drowned. The wounded Columbus leaped into the sea as his ship began to sink. He managed to stay afloat by hanging on to a long oar, and "by a miracle," as he wrote, swam and floated to the Portuguese shore 6 miles (almost 10 km) off. The fisherfolk of Lagos took him in and kept him until he recovered his strength. Soon after, he made his way to Lisbon, the capital city of Portugal, where the Genoese merchants he worked for had offices and agents. By accident, by a stroke of fate, Lisbon would transform his life.

5

The Street Corner
of Europe

It could not have been a happier landing for an adventurous young sailor. In 1476, at the age of twenty-five, Columbus found himself in Portugal, the greatest school of seafaring Europe could offer. Portugal, the almost legendary heart of exploration; Portugal, whose ships sailed down the west coast of Africa or out on the Atlantic to the strange islands dotting the ocean; Portugal, whose mariners had brought home rich cargoes of gold dust, ivory, pepper—and slaves.

Portugal's achievements in shipbuilding, in navigation and astronomy, in discovery and conquest of the unknown, had made it famous throughout Europe for half a century. Her voyagers, as we have seen, dispelled many myths and inspired faith in the ambitious that anything you wanted to do could be done.

When Columbus came to Lisbon, he was penniless and poorly educated. He knew little about the world. His experience on the sea was limited to the Mediterranean and that brief, disastrous voyage into the Atlantic that had ended in near-death. Lisbon became his training ground for the great adventure to come. The city sat on hills above the Tagus, the river whose waters mixed with the ocean. The coast, today dotted with villas, was wild in his time. The brightly painted houses of the city lined the maze of narrow streets jammed with people hurrying about their business. There Columbus entered partnership with his younger

Lisbon, the port Columbus came to in 1476.
The engraving by the Flemish artist Theodore
de Bry was made in the 16th century.

brother Bartholomew, who had come to Lisbon earlier and set up shop to make and sell mariner's charts. Both men had acquired skills in cartography and calligraphy; how, we do not know. (Such details and much more about the years in Lisbon will probably never be found out because the great Lisbon earthquake of 1755 destroyed the documents that may have recorded what Columbus was doing.) Theirs was a thriving business—bringing old charts up to date by putting in the latest information brought home by the seafarers.

Not long after settling in Lisbon, Columbus shipped out, this time to the North Atlantic. Genoese companies operating in Portugal sent out a convoy loaded with merchandise to be sold in Flemish, English, and Icelandic markets. Iceland, the island settled by the Norse long before, was the most distant of all lands known to the map makers. "Thule," they called it, marking it at the very edge of the globe. Columbus reached Iceland and then, he said, sailed a hundred miles (160 km) beyond it. On his way north he had stopped at the English port of Bristol, and on the way back, at Galway in Ireland. Everywhere he went he asked eagerly for what people knew about the Atlantic. In Iceland, so the story goes, he heard the legends of the Norse voyages further west to Greenland and Labrador, and probed eagerly for the details that separate fantasy from reality.

But how could that have been? Did he speak the Icelandic language? Or did he imagine such conversations long after the event, and with the impulse we all share try to make a good story better? His was a vigorous mind, and his spirit welcomed high adventure. His son Ferdinand linked his father with a prophetic passage from the writings of the Roman dramatist Seneca: "An age will come after many years when the ocean will loose the chain of things, and a huge land lie revealed; when Tiphys will disclose new worlds and Thule no more be the ultimate." And had he not already reached this Thule (Iceland)?

What else could he do? Where else could he sail? Everything about Lisbon heated an adventurer's desire to find new and unknown lands. Situated on "the street corner of Europe," Portugal drew merchants, astronomers, cosmographers, mathematicians, geographers, navigators who made their unique contributions to the arts of oceanic discovery. From tiny Portugal would come the knowledge and skills to penetrate the farthest corners of the vast world.

For this was the first European country to give its active support over a long period of time to overseas exploration. Whether it was done with trade or conquest or conversion in mind, the impulse was irresistibly powerful.

Portugal herself did not raise the generation of scholars and scientists who would nourish discovery. That kind of learning was rare in Portugal. The country depended on foreign sources; she borrowed most of the skills she needed. Lisbon housed Italian, German, Arab, and Jewish intellectuals drawn to the small capital by what seemed unlimited opportunity.

One of the most celebrated astronomers of that time was the Portuguese Jew Abraham Zacuto (1452–c. 1515). He developed tables and charts applying theoretical knowledge to the solution of particular problems. His tables of declination helped seamen find latitudes by solar observation. Out of his and others' work came a fixed procedure to enable intelligent and literate seamen to use the tables. Zacuto's pupil José Vizinho was sent in 1485 on a voyage to Guinea to test the new method of latitude-finding by actual observation on the African coast. Through such work came the first European manual of navigation and nautical almanac. The book is extremely detailed because practical sailors did not have the training to grasp the mathematics and astronomy. Before the book became available they acquired what they needed to know by memorizing it.

The manual was a revolutionary advance in the science of navigation. Sailors earlier in the century had no means of finding out their position when they lost sight of land. Which is why they took great care to keep a coastline always in view. But now a navigator had several ways of finding his latitude, and charts on which to plot his observations. (There still was no means of finding longitude; that problem would not be solved until the eighteenth century.)

Columbus learned his navigation during these years in Portugal. He understood how to sail by latitude and to make polestar observations. There is no record, however, of his taking a sun sight (an observation of the sun's altitude), and the experts think he probably did not know how to work one out. His method would be to make careful dead reckoning, and check it, when the weather permitted, by observations of latitude.

There was a great gulf between the intellectual achievements of such a man as Zacuto and what the young and uneducated Columbus knew. It did not intimidate the Genoese. He read whatever he could find, made notes, and thought about the implications of what he was learning. Some of the books he acquired at this time he passed on to his son Ferdinand. Later these were deposited in the Columbus archives in Seville. Scholars today can see the notes in the margins made in the discoverer's own hand.

A few of these books were so important to Columbus that he took them along on his voyages and never lost them. They include *The Book of Marco Polo*, Pliny's *Natural History*, Zacuto's *Perpetual Almanac*, Cardinal d'Ailly's *Imago Mundi*, and Cardinal Piccolomini's *Historia Rerum*. Of course Ptolemy was essential to him, and so was the Bible. Probably he had used or owned a copy of the fifteenth-century handbook which selected from the Bible all the passages on the cosmos and astronomy.

From his readings he jotted down such significant lines as "All seas are navigable," "All seas are peopled by lands," "The Ocean Sea is no emptier than any other," "Every country has its east and west." You can feel his imagination straining to probe the limits of the globe. Many of the ancient writers spoke of other regions, other lands, another world. He absorbed all he could of what the learned men taught while he strained to see beyond their words into the unknown.

It was only a short while before Columbus began reading these books that Gutenberg had made his epochal invention of printing. It was of inestimable value to the spread of knowledge. Like most inventions its origin was complex What Johan Gutenberg of Mainz in Germany did around the year 1450 was to devise movable type, and materials and techniques to establish a workable printshop. New methods of printing and copperplate engraving were combined with the older woodcut tradition to furnish eager audiences with words and images. Book printing and typography developed so swiftly that by 1500 over 1,000 printshops in Europe had produced about 35,000 books in some 10 million copies. There were even a few printers who employed as many as a hundred men.

Printing made it possible for the first time to publish multiple copies that were alike and yet could be spread everywhere. The development of woodcuts and copperplate engravings did for the graphic arts just what printing did for texts. Works of art—as well as maps and charts and tables—could be reproduced exactly and diffused everywhere. The two inventions, printing and engraving, were of vast importance to the growth of knowledge. The mathematical and astronomical tables of Zacuto were published with an exactness that made them dependable for Columbus and all other seafarers.

Printing not only made available to sailors navigational manuals and sailing directions but spread the news of discoveries much faster than manuscripts could do. While much of the writing of the specialists remained in manuscript, such works as Ptolemy's *Geography* were printed before 1500. Printing became "the common mother of all sciences" as it extended knowledge to a wider readership than could ever have been done without printing. The progress of science itself was quickened as new discoveries were published and made the basis for the work of others. While Prince Henry the Navigator knew Marco Polo's *Travels* only in manuscript, Columbus, by the time he was living in Lisbon, was able to acquire a printed copy.

With the humanists' revival of Ptolemy had come the application of mathematic cartography. Seamen continued to use the portolan charts worked out after the compass was introduced in the late 1200s. The first sea charted was the Mediterranean, then the Atlantic coast of Europe, and as the great discoverers did their work, both shores of the North Atlantic were mapped.

A few words about these charts and how they were used. They drew coastlines carefully, giving distances between landmarks. Only those features of the land of interest to seamen as ports or navigational aids were marked. The chart makers placed their lettering on the landward side. This left the sea area open for the essential feature of the portolan, which was a network of fine lines, called rhumbs, radiating from a series of compass roses, giving the points of the compass as they were gradually standardized.

Thus a sailor could work out his approximate course from one place to another by tracing the pertinent rhumbs with the constant compass heading, from one compass rose to the next. These charts were quite accurate for distance and direction, although they couldn't cover large sections of the earth's surface.

In the summer of 1478 Columbus was sent by a Genoese merchant in Lisbon on a voyage out on the Atlantic to buy a large amount of sugar on the island of Madeira, a Portuguese colony. The details of the transaction did not satisfy the sugar merchants, and Columbus had to return with his mission incomplete.

The next year he met the woman he was to marry—Dona Felipa Perestrello e Moniz. They met while attending mass in a chapel in Lisbon which was part of a convent boarding school for the daughters of the local aristocracy. How they courted under the severe social restrictions of that day we do not know. Nor how it happened that an old noble family permitted their daughter to marry a nobody, this foreign-born chart maker who had landed in Portugal by chance. Columbus was twenty-eight when they married, and Dona Felipa about twenty-five. Almost

A geographer of Columbus's time,
working with the new instruments and
improved maps that sailors relied on

nothing about her is known, not even the date of her early death, which seems to have occurred before Columbus left Portugal in 1485. They lived briefly with her mother in Lisbon, then moved to Porto Santo, an island near Madeira where her brother was governor. Their only child, Diego, was born there around 1480.

As guests of the governor they stayed about two years. Columbus was busy as both seaman and merchant. He studied the collection of maps and pilot books gathered by his wife's family, and made his own notes on the winds, waves, and currents along the Atlantic. He saw that the wind always blew from west to east, a crucial observation to be of great value to him later.

Then he had the chance to join a long Atlantic voyage down the African coast to the equator. It was in 1482 or 1483, either on a trading expedition or on a royal ship sent to reinforce the Portuguese garrison on the Guinea coast. The king had recently completed work on a great stone castle at El Mina. It symbolized his sovereignty and protected his nation's trade. Gold had been found in the region, exciting great hopes of untold wealth. Later it would prove to be of minor importance, but now it roused the desire to discover still more new lands with rich gold deposits. Like all the other seafarers, Columbus was not immune to greed. And like them too, he would piously declare the gold would be used to finance more Crusades to liberate the Holy Land from the Moslems.

Meanwhile he learned from this voyage that people could survive in the tropics despite the heat, and that ships sailing the equator did not burn up. He noted plants, animals, and people that no one had described before, yet encountered no monsters such as the legends had fearfully described.

The experience of the long passage to Guinea and back with veteran mariners of Portugal must have taught him much. He learned what supplies were needed for long voyages, and how to store them aboard ship, and what kinds of goods native peoples so different from himself liked to trade for. Watching the handling of caravels in all kinds of weather and seas greatly enriched his seamanship.

6

The Great Enterprise
of the Indies

Home again. What would he do now? Settle into the humdrum existence of a merchant? Easy, for a man who had married into a family with such good connections. Surely he could prosper in merchant shipping and sink comfortably into family life in Lisbon. But was that what he wanted? He was thirty, which in his time meant probably more than half his life was behind him. For a man of humble birth, who felt himself somehow superior, what he had was not enough.

His thoughts turned to what he would later call the great Enterprise of the Indies. To reach Asia by sailing west—that became his passion in life. How he got the idea, where, and exactly when, we do not know. He told no one, and the answers are not recorded in his writings. He did not originate the idea, for he was not the first to think that because the world was round, you could reach the Indies by sailing west. As far back as Aristotle men had believed the world was round. And with the recent revival of Ptolemy's astronomy, every educated person knew the arguments for this belief. Columbus never had to convince anyone the earth was a sphere. His task was rather to convince potential backers of a voyage that the earth's circumference was as small as he thought it to be. (His figure was mistaken.) And that the land distance between Iberia and the Indies was proportionately as great as he supposed it to be. (Again, he was mistaken.)

55

No, what was original about Columbus was that he meant actually to *do* it, to sail west to Asia, not just speculate about it.

Probably Columbus got his idea from a book. He read many of the treatises on the cosmos and geography. They could have stimulated his imagination. Then too, he was a man much given to prophesies. Perhaps when he sailed beyond Iceland (Seneca's Thule), he began to imagine *he* would be the one to discover new worlds, to reveal a huge land on the far side of the Atlantic. He knew that Portuguese sailors had found island after island in the ocean but none had yet reached Asia.

While Columbus lived in Portugal and on the islands he heard of ships picking up exotic driftwood and flotsam that must have come from distant, unknown lands. Stories appeared—but after his own voyages to America—that a caravel sailing from Spain to England had been driven by great storms so far out of its course that it reached islands on the far side of the Atlantic. And when it returned, many months later, with only a few survivors, the pilot secretly made for Columbus a chart showing where he had been. But expert navigators discount it as a practical impossibility.

One of the earliest signs of the maturing plans of Columbus is his exchange of letters with Paolo Toscanelli, a Florentine physician and scientist who accepted Marco Polo's notion that the eastern edge of Asia lay much closer to Portugal than commonly thought. In 1474 Toscanelli sent the king of Portugal a letter stating that there was a shorter way to Asia's spices than going down the African coast. And he enclosed a chart to demonstrate how, marking landfalls along the route so that a ship sailing west from Portugal could identify Asia when it got there. His letter assured the king that there would be "no great spaces of the sea to be passed."

Although Portugal took no action on the basis of this letter, Columbus heard about it. Here was a man of great reputation who also believed that sailing west to Asia was a practical idea.

So he wrote to the Florentine, asking for the particulars. Toscanelli replied, welcoming "thy great and noble ambition to pass over to where the spices grow." And sent along a copy of his letter to the king, together with another sea chart. It was great encouragement.

The trouble with Columbus was that his dream was more real to him than reality. So sure was he that he could do what he dreamed of, that he distorted facts and figures to make them fit the dream. Logic had small place in his thinking. Without going into technical details, it may be enough to say that he convinced himself the ocean was *narrower* than it is, and that Asia was *wider* than it is. He sifted through the literature, the maps, the charts produced by scholars and seafarers from ancient times to his time, and wherever figures differed from his concept, he "corrected" them.

Then, ready with his project and the arguments to support it, he presented the Enterprise of the Indies to the king of Portugal late in 1484. What was Columbus like then? Bartolomé de Las Casas, who wrote the all-important *History of the Indies,* met Columbus in 1500 and gives us this portrait:

> He was more than middling tall; face long and giving an air of authority; aquiline nose, blue eyes, complexion light and tending to bright red; beard and hair red when young, but very soon turned gray from his labors; he was affable and cheerful in speaking . . . eloquent and boasting in his negotiations; he was serious in moderation, affable with strangers, and with members of his household gentle and pleasant, with modest gravity and discreet conversation; and so could easily incite in those who saw him to love him.
>
> In fine, he was most impressive in his port and countenance, a person of great state and authority and worthy of all reverence. He was sober and moderate in eating, drinking, clothing, and footwear; it was com-

*Portrait of Bartolomé de Las Casas,
the Spanish missionary and historian,
and friend of the Columbus family*

monly said that he spoke cheerfully in familiar conversation, or with indignation when he gave reproof or was angry with somebody. . . .

Without doubt he was Catholic and of great devotion. . . . he was extraordinarily zealous for the divine service; he desired and was eager for the conversion of these people [the Indians], and that in every region the faith of Jesus Christ be planted and enhanced. And he was especially affected and devoted to the idea that God should deem him worthy of aiding somewhat in recovering the Holy Sepulchre. . . .

A self-taught man, not brilliant, Columbus would be up against far better-educated authorities. But he was doggedly persistent in going after what he wanted. It took courage to approach patrons in those ten years before his enterprise was accepted. Knowing how much better informed they were, he could expect disdain and even ridicule. So he tried to avoid particulars, for there he could be readily challenged. He stuck to generalities, brushing off the details as minor matters to be handled in good time. Some historians think the learned advisors to the kings he approached probably believed Columbus was hiding valuable information, reluctant to disclose it lest others use the knowledge to compete with him. He never did specify the places he meant to find, except to speak vaguely of "islands and mainland in the ocean sea."

He set about finding a private investor or a government to back him. He made his first approach to the king of Portugal. It was a ripe moment, for the nation's enthusiasm for exploration was at its height. The young King John II had recently appointed a committee of experts to improve instruments and charts for exploration and discovery. His mariner Diogo Cão had just returned to Lisbon from a voyage to Africa, where he had explored the Congo River for some distance and brought back several Congolese natives to be instructed in the Christian faith, and was about to leave on a second voyage.

Columbus knew the king was exploring the coast of Africa with the intention of going by that route to Asia. He urged instead that John give him ships to reach Asia by sailing west on the Atlantic. A Portuguese chronicler tells us about their meeting. The king, observing Columbus "to be a big talker and boastful in setting forth his accomplishments, and full of fancy and imagination with his Isle Cypango [Japan] than certain whereof he spoke, gave him small credit."

But so insistent was Columbus that the king asked him to confer with three of his advisers in cosmography and discovery. Result? They all considered the words of Columbus "as vain, simply founded on imagination, or things like that Isle Cypango of Marco Polo." They rejected his proposal, probably because from what they knew, his estimate of the distance to be sailed across the Atlantic was incredibly small. By his calculations the world's circumference was 10 percent smaller than Ptolemy said it was, and (we know now) 25 percent smaller than the real world is. Columbus thus placed Japan 2,400 nautical miles (4,500 km) west of the Canary Islands, which is about where the Virgin Islands sit in the Atlantic. (The true airline distance from the Canaries westward to Japan is 26,600 nautical miles, or 49,300 km.)

Despite the turndown, something about this Genoese adventurer intrigued King John; they remained friendly. Two years later John sent two of his subjects out on the Atlantic to search for islands legend held to be there. That mission failed. Then Bartholomew Dias sailed from Portugal to see if he could find a way around Africa to India. He pushed further down the coast than anyone had gone and managed to round the Cape of Good Hope. But after what seemed endless months at sea, his crew refused to go on. He had to return home.

Columbus, meanwhile, had gone to Spain to try his luck. His wife had died, and he took his five-year-old son, Diego, with him. His brother Bartholomew stayed in Lisbon to run their map business. Columbus landed at the seaport town of Palos and placed his boy nearby, at a Franciscan monastery. He went on to Seville to see Father Antonio de Marchena, the astronomer, and submitted his project for judgment. Father Antonio thought it was a sound idea, and upon his advice Columbus applied to the wealthy duke of Medina Sidonia for support. The duke liked the project, but before he could act, some private quarrel made him abandon it. Columbus turned next to the count of Medina Celi, a major shipowner. The nobleman wanted to finance the enterprise but felt it needed approval first from Queen Isabella of Spain.

After reviewing the proposal, the queen turned it over to an advisory committee. While waiting for their decision Columbus lived in the royal city of Cordova. There he met a young woman named Beatriz Enriquez de Harana, the daughter of a peasant family. Again, as with his wife, Dona Felipa, we know almost nothing about Beatriz except that she could read and write. They did not marry, but in 1488 she bore him a son, Ferdinand.

Beatriz outlived Columbus by fourteen years; how long they stayed together is uncertain. He did not marry her probably because, unlike Dona Felipa, whose high social position helped him get on in the world, Beatriz not only could do nothing for him, but would be a handicap in his Great Enterprise. There was no secret about their affair or their son's birth; it did not matter in a day when kings, nobles, and bishops were open about their mistresses and their illegitimate children. Members of the Harana family would hold important posts with Columbus later, when he embarked on his voyages.

In 1486 Ferdinand and Isabella came to Cordova to take up summer residence in the Alcazar. Columbus was summoned to an audience with the queen. She heard him out, then asked her advisors to look into several questions. Could a voyage west to Asia really be carried out? Could or should the crown pay for it? Or was it better to let Medina Celi underwrite the project?

Los principes muy eccelletes de castilla y de aragon.

While the experts deliberated, Columbus would be in the care of the queen's financial comptroller, Alonso de Quintilla.

The committee, led by Father Fernando de Talavera, the queen's confessor, met at Cordova that summer and then moved with the court to the university town of Salamanca. There professors of geography, mathematics, and astronomy queried Columbus and studied his arguments, then concluded that what he said could not possibly be true. It was contrary to everything they knew. What they meant was that his notion of the distance between Spain and Asia was wrong. The Atlantic was certainly not that narrow.

Of course they could not prove their case. So little was known about the circumference of the earth, the proportion of land to water on its surface, the size of Asia, that it was a matter of one opinion against another. Did Cipango (or Japan) really exist? The only "evidence" was a hearsay report by Marco Polo. And where were the hard figures for the case Columbus made? It rested on prophesies, hints at secret information, guesswork. But this Genoese was so *sure* of himself, so persistent, so persuasive. . . .

Maybe that is why, negative as it felt, the committee put off a final report, and the queen gave Columbus an annual retainer. Not much—the pay of an able seaman—but enough to keep him going (or waiting).

What held matters up even more than the arguments about the Enterprise was the crown's war against the Moors.

Until very recently, Spain had consisted of several small kingdoms. But when Ferdinand, the king of Aragon, married Isabella, the queen of Castile, Spain became united. From 1479

An artist imagines Columbus making his appeal for support to Ferdinand and Isabella.

on, the two jointly ruled the entire country. Except, that is, for Granada. That region was the last remnant of the Moorish Empire. In the eighth century the Moors had swept across North Africa, crossed the straits of Gibraltar, and moved up to establish themselves on the peninsula. Over the centuries the Moorish Empire broke up into petty kingdoms, and the Christians warring against them took back more and more of the land. When Ferdinand and Isabella become dominant as the "Catholic Monarchs," their first goal was to oust the last of the Moors from Granada.

So, intriguing as the Enterprise of Columbus seemed, at this moment it could be of only minor concern to a kingdom devoted to war. Tired of waiting, in 1488 Columbus asked the king of Portugal if he could renew his appeal for support. The king told him to come at once. As Columbus arrived in Lisbon, the three caravels of Dias sailed grandly into the Tagus. Dias reported to King John that Africa really could be rounded by sea: the eastern route to Asia was open. After all the investment Portugal had made in trying to find the route to Asia by sailing south around Africa, she seemed on the very edge of success. What need, then, did the king have for the Grand Enterprise of Columbus?

Columbus returned to Spain. The queen's committee finally recommended, in 1490, that Columbus's proposals be rejected. They didn't believe it was practicable. They did not say so, but it was also a bad time to invest heavily in a dubious project of discovery while the holy war for the conquest of Granada was going on. Through his brother, Columbus approached England and France for support, but they were not ripe for that kind of venture. They had not yet developed the spirit and resources for such projects.

Columbus had no choice but to hope that once the Moors were defeated, Isabella would come round. She kept him dangling on the royal payroll and let him appear at court. Early in 1492 the turn came: the Moors surrendered; this was his great opportunity. But soon after, he got another and seemingly final no.

What had gone wrong? Perhaps Columbus had demanded too much. His arrogance was notorious. He never acted like a weaver's son petitioning royalty, but like an equal. Then came an abrupt change of mind by Isabella. It happened through the hearty support Columbus had won from a powerful figure in the court, Luis de Santangel. He talked the queen into backing Columbus by offering to find at least half the necessary money. He would borrow some of it from the police force he served as treasurer, some would come from his own personal wealth, and Columbus himself would come up with funds, probably borrowed from Italian investors.

With money no longer the troublesome issue, the queen said yes. A bold and imaginative woman, she could not resist so dramatic a project, and the magnetic personality of Columbus appealed to her. Reluctantly, because the queen wanted it, Ferdinand went along.

7

Three Ships
and
Ninety Men

Everything Columbus asked for, the queen agreed to. He wanted enormous rewards if his Enterprise should succeed. As one historian suggests, he succeeded more on his salesmanship than his seamanship. Salesmen learn that if you price yourself high, the buyer believes you're worth a lot.

What did he ask for? Ten percent of all the wealth that would pour into Spain from his new route to Asia. Not only the riches he would personally bring in, but all that everyone else might gather, and for all time, for both himself and his heirs. He asked to be given the title of viceroy, and Admiral of the Ocean Sea, together with other honors. The title of admiral would give him command of the western Atlantic and a share in all the naval booty to be drawn from that vast region.

To the Spanish monarchs this didn't seem outrageous. What did they have to lose? Others were paying for a large portion of the Enterprise expenses. And 10 percent of whatever wealth Columbus might find still left 90 percent to Their Majesties.

So in April 1492 the terms of agreement were signed.

Columbus got his fleet and the command he asked for. The fleet was rather modest: three ships—his flagship, the *Santa María*, a tubby cargo carrier; and two smaller trading caravels, the square-rigged *Pinta* and the lateen-rigged *Niña*. The *Santa María* was chartered for the voyage, but the two smaller ships

A woodcut of the fleet. From left,
the Santa Maria, *the* Pinta, *and the* Niña.

were commandeered from their owners by the town of Palos, which had been ordered by the crown to provide two vessels for Columbus as a fine for smuggling in goods from West Africa. The *Santa María* was around 100 tons, the *Pinta* and the *Niña,* perhaps 60 tons each. (Not till a century later would the great galleons of a thousand tons and more appear.)

To give some idea of dimensions, the *Niña,* according to recent research, was probably 67 feet (20.4 m) long, with a beam of 21 feet (6.4 m), and a draft of about 7 feet (2.1 m.) She could carry about 60 tons of cargo. Although the smallest ship of the fleet, she carried four masts. The ships were steered by an outboard rudder and a large wooden tiller. (The steering wheel would not be invented until the eighteenth century.)

Like the other ships on the great voyages of discovery, these vessels were not specially designed for their task. They were meant for the coastwise trade, and there were few guns aboard and no soldiers. The explorers expected to be welcomed into the ports of the great kingdoms of Asia, so why carry weapons? Except for the familiar enemy, the Moslems of the Levant, their only experience with non-European peoples had come in the Canaries and West Africa. And there they had met small trouble from native chieftains. Perhaps they expected the Christianizing part of their mission to assure them a peaceable reception.

The *Niña* belonged to Juan Niño, who would make the voyage with Columbus. The *Pinta,* built in the Palos shipyards, was commanded by Martín Alonso Pinzón, a shipowner and a famous seafarer with far more experience than Columbus (who had never commanded a ship). The two men, who had met earlier, were matched in arrogance, a fact that would cause trouble later. But now Pinzón's prestige was of great help in recruiting the crews, some of whom came from the Pinzón and the Niño families. The *Santa María,* built in Galicia and originally called *La Gallega,* was rented from its owner, Juan de la Cosa, who went along as its master. It was a squat ship with greater draft than the others, and less swift and manageable. Columbus re-named it the *Santa María*, in devout homage to the saint.

We do not know exactly what these three caravels looked like, for no drawings or paintings have been found which depict any of the vessels. But replicas have been constructed on the basis of scraps of evidence, the knowledge of other caravels of the period, and plain guesswork. (I went aboard the replica of the *Santa María*, which is docked in the harbor at Barcelona, and was amazed at how tiny it appears to the eye in this day of huge freighters and ocean liners and battleships.)

The *Santa María*, like the other two ships, had one deck, with sails, ropes, masts, and water pumps and ballast kegs strewn over it. The stern held a small cabin for Columbus and an even smaller room below housed an officer or two. The forecastle was a small storeroom for other equipment. The sailors had no sleeping quarters but the steerage, or the open deck in good weather. Food was cooked on an open firebox, sand spread on its floor and a wood fire built on it. Life aboard ship was miserably uncomfortable. The caravels were too small to carry the crew, the gear, the provisions, the water, and the trading goods for long voyages. Yet these small ships were versatile and reliable.

The crew of the flagship numbered forty men; the *Niña* had twenty-four and the *Pinta*, twenty-six. The working conditions were terrible. It took hard and constant labor to man a sailing vessel. Wooden ships leaked badly. Although the drainage pumps were in constant use, the bilge gave off an overpowering stink.

Almost all the names of the ninety men are recorded in the Spanish archives, where their pay too is given. The officers got 2,000 maravedis a month, the sailors half that, and the ship's boys still less. Part of their pay the men drew in advance, with the rest to be paid on their return. They needed no cash aboard ship: there was nothing to buy. Except for Columbus and a few others, all the crewmen were Spanish.

The officers on each ship were captain, master, and pilot. The captain had ultimate responsibility for everyone and everything; Columbus commanded the entire fleet as well as the flagship. The master gave orders to the seamen and supervised all the details of running a ship. The pilot took charge of the navigation and kept the daily record of the ship's position.

The specialists carried by the fleet included an interpreter, who knew Hebrew and some Arabic and was expected somehow to be able to converse with the Asians they would encounter; a marshal, or disciplinary officer, on each ship; a secretary to keep the voyage's journal and record any diplomatic proceedings; and a comptroller to watch expenses and record the riches of whatever kind they would gather. Each vessel had a so-called surgeon to care for the sick or wounded. Among the petty officers were boatswain, steward, carpenter, cooper, caulker, and painter.

The fleet carried no cooks. Columbus had his personal servant to prepare his meals. Perhaps the ship's boys cooked for the seamen. The food was probably much like that of laborers and peasants ashore: beef or pork packed in brine, barreled salt fish, fresh fish caught at sea in calm weather, and ship's biscuit for bread. There was also cheese, onions, garlic, dried peas and beans, and chick-peas. The biggest problem on long voyages was drinking water. It was stored in casks and quickly went foul. So wine was carried too, doled out to the crew in daily allowances.

The specialists or craftsmen and the seamen who worked under their direction displayed great skills at improvisation. They were able to carry out major repairs of damage suffered at sea, and to do it even in violent weather, using whatever materials could be found. If a ship had been wrecked on some strange coast, they sometimes managed to build new ships out of the salvaged wreckage and local timber. Their workmanship and inventiveness is a marvel to us today.

So Columbus would embark with good ships, capable officers, and experienced seamen. But he himself had somewhat shaky qualifications. He had never commanded a ship, much less a fleet. This was a Spanish enterprise, and he was Genoese, which would not have made him popular with the Spanish crew. Nor would they like taking orders from a man of such humble birth. That he was aware of these handicaps may account, in part, for his secretiveness. He would rarely confide in his officers. But with the queen's backing, and his own powerful will, he would exert the necessary authority.

It took some months to get the ships ready and to sign on the ninety men ready to risk their lives. The date of departure was set for Friday, August 3, 1492. The three ships would sail down the River Tinto, out of Palos.

Why Palos? It was a small port, nothing like Cádiz, the principal Spanish port on the Atlantic. But Cádiz was tied up by other business of Their Majesties. Ferdinand and Isabella had signed an edict prepared by the Holy Inquisition, calling for the Jews to be expelled from Spain. August 2 had been fixed as the deadline for the last Jew to leave. Any Jews found thereafter would be executed unless they converted to Catholicism. So for the crime of holding fast to their faith, 8,000 people were on that day penned up in the holds of all kinds of ships departing from Cádiz. To where? To whatever place in Christian Europe would accept them, or to the more tolerant countries of Islam. Most went to North Africa, to northern Italy, or to Holland.

Behind the expulsion of the Jews lay Spain's move toward political unity, which in that time meant religious unity. The monarchs had finally succeeded in conquering the last Moslems and driving them out; now it was the Jews' turn to go.

Persecution of the Jews
during the Inquisition

In his journal Columbus mentions that his voyage was allowed to start only after Spain had been purged of Jews. His mission—apart from the hunt for gold—was to extend the Catholic domain by converting the heathen of Asia to "our Holy Faith."

On the evening of August 2, the men went to mass to say their last prayers before boarding ship. Who could have slept well that night? Tomorrow they would leave for the vast unknown, on a course no ship had ever charted before them. What would they find on the far side of the ocean?

They did not know their voyage would change the world.

8

Land! Land!

On August 3, the day of his departure from Palos, Columbus began to keep a careful log of his voyage. It runs to March 15, 1493. Much of what we know about the voyage comes from this source, although it hasn't come down to us in its original form. Upon his return, copies were made by Ferdinand and Isabella for their experts to study. What happened to the original, we don't know. But upon the death of Columbus one copy was acquired by Diego, his eldest son, who let Las Casas, friend of Columbus and the first historian of the Indies, read the log and copy the most important passages. Diego's own copy disappeared later, and so Las Casas's book—which in part quotes and in part summarizes the log—is the only source we now have. (None of the logs written on the later voyages survive.)

Columbus set his course south to make the Canary Islands his first port. From there he would sail due west. Why the Canaries? Because of all the islands off Europe, they were the only Spanish colony. That made them a good staging place for the long leap beyond. Earlier, while sailing down the coast of Africa, Columbus had observed the northeast trade winds that blow steadily over the ocean at the latitude of the Canaries. This wind, he hoped, would drive his ships to his goal. And that goal—Japan—was on the same latitude—28 degrees north—as the Canaries, he thought. (He was off somewhat: Japan lies 10 de-

*In de Bry's illustrated collection of voyages he
pictures Columbus's farewell to Ferdinand and Isabella
as the fleet sets out from Palos on August 3, 1492.*

grees farther north.) So if he kept to the 28th parallel and sailed west, in a few weeks' time he would land in Japan (less than 3,000 miles, or 4,800 km, away, he wrongly estimated).

In about ten days the fleet reached the Canaries, where some refitting of the ships was done, and water, wood and provisions taken abroad. The *Pinta,* with a badly damaged rudder, had fallen far behind, but it came in at last and was repaired. On September 6 the fleet unfurled the sails and headed straight out into the unknown.

The sea was calm, the air mild, the sky at sunset brilliant, and the trade winds blew unchangingly in the right direction. They girdle the globe at the tropical latitudes, with slight shifts higher or lower as the seasons change. Columbus had only hints of this phenomenon of nature from his African voyage. Luckily the hopes he pinned on the wind pattern were realized.

What speed the fleet made he could only guess at; the log line had not yet been invented. The compass gave him the course. Time was measured with the sands of the hourglass. Putting estimated speed, course, and time together gave him a rough measure of the fleet's position. It was the method of dead reckoning, and Columbus had a great gift for it.

As soon as the last of the Canaries had dropped from view, the men began to feel an inevitable tension. As the days passed, the unease heightened. None had ever been out of sight of land for so long. And with the wind blowing steadily from the northeast, would they be able to sail back home against it? The worry lessened when they sailed into strong southwesterly seas one day. These westerlies, Columbus said, would bless their passage home.

Still, he knew how nervous the men were, and how fearful of unpredictable disaster. To keep the crews' spirits up, each day when he estimated the number of miles sailed, he put down distances less than he made, "so that if the voyage were long," he wrote, "the people would not be frightened or dismayed." His deception turned out to be not that great, for he tended to overestimate distances sailed. The false reckoning he gave the men was actually close to the facts.

A few days beyond the Canaries the men sighted birds flying out of the west, opposite to their direction. Heron, albatross, sea eagle, sea swallow: were they a sign of land nearby? A week later, even more birds. (These were North American birds on their annual autumn migration to the West Indies via Bermuda.) Perhaps the fleet was nearing one of those mythical islands of the Atlantic? And then fish too appeared, as the ocean's color shifted from blue to violet. The fish were big, with long tapered bodies. The sailors caught a few and found them tasty.

In mid-September they sailed into immense patches of sargasso weed, "great banks of very green grass," noted the log, "that looks as though it was just recently cut from the earth. We all figured that we must be near an island." Did it mean they were nearing their goal? But day after day the horizon was layered over with this floating bright green and yellow gulfweed until the sailors feared its thickness would cripple the fleet's passage. They insisted the commander change course, but Columbus plowed straight ahead.

And then another alarming event: the compass's magnetic needle began moving toward northwest. Columbus had ordered the ships to steer due west; was the helmsman doing a poor job of steering? Intuitively, Columbus realized this was not human error but a magnetic inclination toward some other point away from the North Star. By regular observation of the North Star's position he realized that geographical north does not coincide with magnetic north. Allowing for this, he avoided letting his fleet sail far to the north, where it might have been lost forever.

After scudding along under the trade winds the fleet encountered long lulls. The ships could barely crawl ahead. The crew began to grumble and make nasty remarks about this Genoese who had got them into such a mess. They did not know it, but at this point they had sailed only a third of the way. Yet that was twice as far as the distance from Palos to the Azores or the

*Artists of that time fantasized about the
strange creatures of air and ocean that ships
might encounter on voyages of discovery.
This is one of de Bry's visions.*

Cape Verde Islands, the farthest any of them had ever gone before.

The drifting continued for days, until on September 22 a head wind rose up. It blew from the southwest and lasted several days. At least it showed the sailors there were winds capable of bringing the ships back to Spain. When the wind died away, huge, heavy waves turned the ocean surface into great hills and valleys. The caravels rode to their heights then plunged into the hollows. This was the tail end of storms perhaps hundreds of miles off. To Columbus it was a sign of God's favor: "A miracle of this sort," he wrote in the log, "has not come to pass since the Egyptians took to pursuing Moses and the Jews he had freed from slavery."

God's assurance pleased Columbus but could do little to calm the men's fears. Twenty days on the Atlantic had passed: where was the promised land? Columbus had Pinzón come aboard the flagship for a consultation. Pinzón's task was to take care of the technical aspects of the voyage, which meant the crews' morale too. The two men went over a map, which may have been a copy of Toscanelli's map, a hypothetical construct of the world of little practical use here. Whatever they saw on the map, they emerged from their session talking about islands that should be located close by. The next day they pointed out to the men dim outlines of something to the southwest that looked like an island, perhaps only 30 miles (48 km) away. The sailors raced up the masts to spy it out, but it proved to be only sky, not land.

How the crews felt after this letdown we don't know. Columbus only notes how weary they were. The fleet inched ahead, for the sea had again become dead calm. During the first week of October the ships picked up speed. Intending to go due west, the fleet was slowly trending southward. Flocks of petrels flew over, but with no land in sight, the men wondered: had they somehow missed Cipango and gone past it, moving toward the Asiatic mainland? A month at sea had gone by. It seemed mad to drag along without knowing where the fleet was going or when, if ever, it would get there.

Early on October 7, as the *Niña* was sailing in advance of the fleet, she broke out a flag and fired a gun, signaling land ahead—another false landfall. (The nearest land was 370 miles, or 595 km, away.) At sunset, Columbus changed the fleet's course to west-southwest when he saw great flights of birds heading to the southwest. He remembered that the Portuguese had found the Azores by observing the movement of birds. So he decided to steer by them, rather than by his chart.

The next few days, with the air as soft and fragrant as April in Seville, the fleet kept steady to the west-southwest course, flocks of birds arrowing over them. But on October 10, with no land yet in sight and the fleet having long since passed the place where Columbus had assured them land would be found, the men rebelled. They would stand it no longer! Columbus replied it was useless to complain; he was on his way to the Indies and he would not stop until he found them, "with the help of Our Lord."

Some sailors said Columbus promised the men he would turn back if land was not sighted in the next few days. Other sailors testified many years later that Columbus himself lost confidence, or was so dismayed by the men's mutinous mood, he proposed to turn back, and that it was only the Pinzón group that persuaded him to keep going.

Whatever the truth of these stories, the fleet did move on. Then, on October 11, a gale blew up and the ships raced ahead. Now there were unmistakable signs of land nearby—floating branches, sticks, great flocks of birds crossing the sky, with some dropping down to the ships and singing in the rigging. On the wind the sailors could catch the scent of flowers and herbs.

Very early on the morning of October 12, 1492, Rodrigo de Triana, a sailor aboard the *Pinta,* the fastest ship and out in the lead, called out "Land! Land!" He had seen the moon shining on the cliffs and lighting the sandy beach of an island.

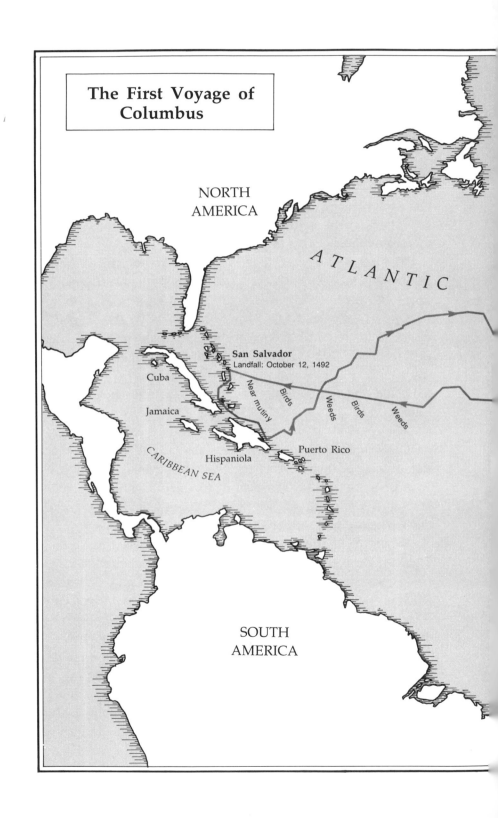

The First Voyage of Columbus

NORTH
AMERICA

ATLANTIC

San Salvador
Landfall: October 12, 1492

Cuba

Jamaica

Near mutiny

Birds

Weeds

Birds

Weeds

Puerto Rico

Hispaniola

CARIBBEAN SEA

SOUTH
AMERICA

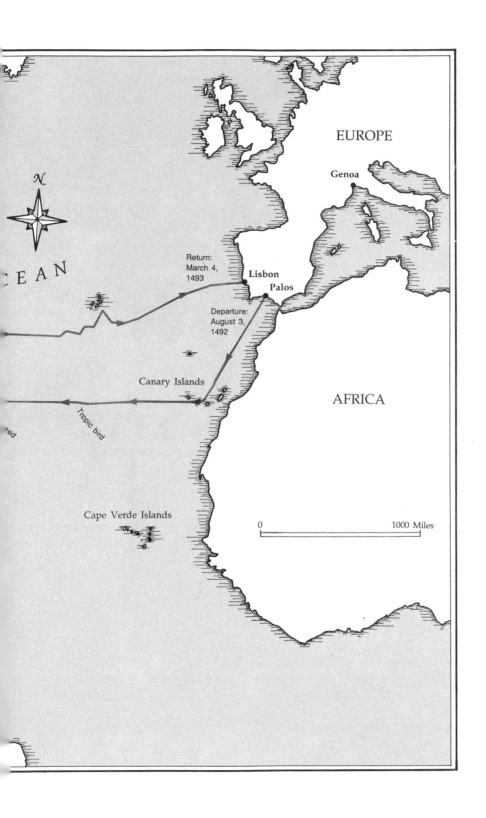

As the first person to sight land, Rodrigo was due the promised royal reward of 10,000 maravedis annually for the rest of his life. But Columbus claimed to have seen a light the evening before, and therefore the reward was *his*. Whether the admiral did this injustice to a sailor out of greed or the desire to take all the glory to himself, it does him little honor.

It was the first land of the western hemisphere to be sighted by Europeans since the Norse voyages. It was the eastern shore of one of the Bahamas, an island the natives called Guanahani and Columbus named San Salvador—Holy Savior. But exactly which of the 700-odd islands of the Bahamas was it? For several hundred years geographers and cartographers argued over it. Nine different islands were proposed as San Salvador. The two most frequently chosen were Watlings and Samana. Finally, in 1986, after the *National Geographic* put together a large team of specialists to study the issue, the magazine reported that Samana was its finding. It matched most closely the description of Columbus.

The coral island is about 13 miles (21 km) long and 6 miles (10 km) wide, with dangerous reefs surrounding it. The fleet groped its way around to the western side, where it found an opening through the reef barrier and dropped anchor. On the shore the men saw "naked people" coming down to look at these strange ships and beings. Columbus and the captains of the other ships went ashore in small boats, flying the royal expedition's banners. They kneeled down on the earth, "embracing it with tears of joy," wrote Las Casas, "for the immeasurable mercy of having reached it." Then, with his men as witness, "and in the presence of many natives of that land assembled together," Columbus "took possession of that island in the name of the Catholic sovereigns. . . . Many Indians having come together for that ceremony and rejoicing, the Admiral, seeing that they were a gentle and peaceful people and of great simplicity, gave them some little red caps and glass beads which

One of the best-known paintings of Columbus and his crew landing in the Americas. Done by the American John Vanderlyn in the mid-1800s, it hangs in the Rotunda of the Capitol in Washington, D.C.

they hung around their necks, and other things of slight worth, which they all valued at the highest price.''

He had ''discovered'' what Europeans would soon call the New World of the Americas. But not Columbus, who mistakenly thought he had landed on islands of the Indies, off the coast of Asia, and therefore called these native people Indians.

Nor was it a New World to the millions of dark-skinned Native Americans. They had been there thousands of years before the white man would ''discover'' them, enslave them, and exterminate them.

9

The People of
the New World

The landing of Columbus on that tiny island would have devastating effects upon the life of the Native Americans. And what the Europeans would do in and with the New World would in turn greatly change life in the Old World.

Who were the people Columbus found living in the New World? The first of them had arrived in the Americas from Asia during the last Ice Age, when glaciers covered much of the northern hemisphere. As modern man in his present form, *Homo sapiens,* they developed elsewhere and then entered the New World. They probably found an ice-free passage, a grassy treeless plain, that once connected Siberia with Alaska. The animals that lived on that plain drew hunters down from Asia. These hunters in search of prey were the ancestors of the Indians and the first people to explore North America. Over something like 25,000 years they spread from the far north to the southernmost tip of South America. Their descendants sometimes gave up the nomadic life and settled down. They came to the Americas before the dog was domesticated, before the bow and arrow were invented. They knew fire, they roasted meat, they probably wore skins. They moved through several stages of development before Columbus arrived. From hunting and gathering food, some turned to farming, some took up trading, and some built complex cultures and great cities, creating art, architecture, astronomy, and mathematics that would become world-renowned.

Columbus knew nothing about them of course. He did not realize they were not a single people but many different people. It is estimated that there were 25 million or more Indians then in South America, and about 4 million in North America. Partly because they were so few in number, and spread over vast areas, they had developed hundreds of different societies. In physical appearance, in culture, in language, they varied as widely as the people who lived in the Old World.

But Columbus and most of the white explorers and colonizers who would come after him were not able to see that. They saw the natives through a European looking glass; the image was badly distorted. The whites would debate whether the Indians were human. Some would say the Indians were a sort of two-legged animal without soul or spirit. If the Indians were subhuman, then the white need have no qualms about his treatment of them.

Unable to understand the Indians, the Europeans would call them savages or barbarians. (Every people has found it hard to appreciate the customs, culture, and religion of another people. It was true of the Egyptians, the Greeks, the Romans, the Chinese. It is still true.) But it can surely be supposed that the Indians thought of themselves as civilized. They lived by what their society believed to be true and good goals. The way they behaved was shaped by the values of their society, values they consciously respected. Who is savage and who is civilized? To Columbus, confident of his own people's superiority, the answer was obvious.

What the people of the Americas were like then is much better understood today than 500 years ago. Most of us picture the Indian with high cheekbones, an eagle-beak nose, and reddish-brown skin. But the Indians were not a uniform group when Columbus came. Some scientists believe that the Native Americans were the result of the ancient intermingling of ethnic groups.

Or at first they may have been a relatively uniform people, who developed into separate groups through isolation, genetic change, and intermixture. It is thought that there were some 2,000 different languages spoken by the people of the New World.

The Indians were divided not only by language and culture but by physical appearance. One group might be heavily bearded and round-faced, while another might be lightly bearded and sharp-featured. From one region to another of this vast hemisphere, many variations in color, eye, nose, height, build could be found. Great differences sometimes occurred even among Indians who lived not far from one another.

Some Indians lived in well-built houses of logs, planks, or adobe, some in many-roomed longhouses of bark, some in earth lodges, some in multistoried communal pueblos. Many lived in towns or villages. Only some, such as the nomadic hunters of the plains, used the hide-covered tepee that most moviegoers think of as the typical Indian dwelling.

The Indians provided for their family and their tribe by hunting, fishing, or farming. The men usually did the hunting and fishing, and made the tools and weapons. The women—with exceptions in some places—raised the crops, cooked, made the clothes, took care of the children. The Indians sought to have enough to live on, not to get rich.

The Indians knew how to grow plants, and they steadily improved upon them by seed selection, by soil culture, and by the use of fertilizers. The whites would learn to grow corn properly from the Indians. Indian farmers raised sweet potatoes, tomatoes, pumpkins, peanuts, squash, chili peppers, beans, and many other crops. They would introduce tobacco to the Europeans. Indians developed cotton independently from efforts to raise it in the Old World. They devised complex irrigation systems that made farming possible in desert regions.

Metals such as bronze, iron, and steel were unknown to the Indians. The tools they used for farming, fishing, hunting, and war were made of stone, bone, or wood. Indian clothing was usually made of hides or furs, with moccasins the chief footgear.

The forms of Indian life before the whites came were as richly varied as the language and cultural patterns. The rigid social structures of the Aztecs and Mayas were unknown north of Central America. Most Indian societies did not hold war to be their principal objective. War among the Indians was nothing like the Old World wars conducted by armies ruled by military leaders. Indian raids were usually made on the initiative of an individual, and involved only a small part of the men and for a short time. Some tribes warred against each other and some joined forces as allies. The defeated were assimilated, not annihilated, or there was a negotiated truce, with the fighters returning home. But there were Indian groups who did not approve of war and would fight only when attacked. Theirs was the spirit of quietness and peace.

A basic difference between the world of Columbus and the Indian world was the way they viewed property. The Europeans generally believed in individual competition to acquire property. The Indian attitude was to cooperate in the use of property held in common. They did not compete to acquire private property. No Indian had the exclusive right to own or use a piece of land, to give it away or to sell it. That was a concept the whites would bring which the Indians would not understand. To the Indians the land was for all. They had a reverence for the earth and its web of life. They saw humanity as linked to the universe, partner in its vitality.

As William Brandon puts it, "The Indian world was devoted to living, while the European world was devoted to getting." And that difference, he suggests, was what made inevitable the collapse of the Indian world when it collided with a materialistic civilization.

That first day in the West Indies, Columbus noted in his journal what struck him about these strange people:

They all go as naked as their mothers bore them, and
the women also. . . . Some of them paint their faces,
some their whole bodies, some only the nose. They do
not bear arms or know them, for I showed to them swords
and they took them by the blade and cut themselves
through ignorance. These people are very unskilled in
arms. . . . With fifty men they could all be subjected
and made to do all that I wished.

Their generous ways puzzled him:

Anything they have, if it be asked for they never say
no, but rather invite the person to accept it, and show
as much lovingness as though they would give their
hearts. . . .

Nor have I ever been able to learn whether they
held personal property, for it seemed to me that whatever one had, they all took shares of. . . .

Columbus and the Indians looked curiously, and warily, upon
one another. The whites did not know what to make of the Indians, nor were the Indians sure of who and what the whites
were. The tendency of the whites was to treat the Indians like
animals, while, for their part, the Indians wondered if the whites
might be gods.

For the most part the Indians of the West Indies were peaceful people. Now they collided with Spaniards bent on conquest
of the Americas. Trained up as a warrior class during the civil
wars in Spain between Christians and Moslems, the Spaniards
came to the New World fired with religious zeal and a great lust
for wealth. The Spaniards believed there was only one God in
heaven, and Their Catholic Majesties were here on earth to rule
it. The natives they would meet must become subjects of the
crown and serve it.

*For a 1493 printing of the Columbus letter,
an artist visualizes the Indians fleeing at
the sight of the Spanish ships.*

The idea that the Indians might have a right to determine their own way of life and to govern themselves never occurred to Columbus. His mission was to bring them under the authority of God and Spain, peacefully if he could, by the sword if necessary. Although he believed he was in the realm of some Asian ruler, he did not hesitate to proclaim that he was taking possession of these lands for the king and queen of Spain. Again, from his journal:

They [the Indians] would make fine servants, and they are intelligent, for I saw that they repeated everything said to them. I believe they could easily be made Christians, for they appeared to have no idols. God willing, when I make my departure I will bring half a dozen back to Their Majesties. . . . Should Your Majesties command it, all the inhabitants could be taken away to Castile, or made slaves on the island.

Here Columbus is opening the door to the conversion of untold numbers of people to Christianity. He puts himself forward as a soldier of the faith, a redeemer of souls. And with this image of himself he justified all the consequences of his Great Enterprise.

One of those consequences he brings up himself almost immediately: enslavement. These innocent and trusting Indians could easily be made not only good Christians but "fine servants," by which he meant slaves.

That evening Columbus and his men returned to the fleet. In the morning they sailed out to explore the island, but seeing little of interest—no spices, no silks, no rugs—turned south, where the natives had said he would find more islands. San Salvador must be at the northern tip of the chain of islands his maps said were close to Cipango. Now he would go find Cipango itself.

The fleet twisted through the Bahamas, fearful of coral reefs and shallows, stopping at many islands. Here Columbus showed his great aptitude for sensing new conditions and adjusting to them. He quickly grasped the way land and sea breezes functioned in these islands, with the wind reversal that comes with the varied heating and cooling of the land and water. Veteran navigators of the Bahamas marvel at how he managed to avoid a major disaster, considering that he had no charts, there were no lighthouses, and he knew no landmarks to guide him.

As the fleet moved along, Columbus found all the natives looking much the same, eager to trade food for beads, bits of cloth, tiny bells. He had a keen eye for whatever he came across, as his notes reveal. He liked the Caribbean climate and the respectful and peaceable natives. He noted many new plants and shrubs and guessed they might prove to be useful sources of dyes, medicines, and spices. But he had no way to identify them. The crew gathered some cinnamon, aloes, and aromatic resins. And the manmade hammock too—"beds similar to cotton nets and made like suspenders." They made for comfortable sleeping, and the crew took several along to use on the ships.

When Luis de Torres, the interpreter in the crew who knew Arabic, tried to speak to the Indians, none understood him. This seemed odd to Columbus, for he thought Arabic was a common language in the Indies. Always Columbus asked, Where is the gold? And never did anyone have any. By gesture, they told Columbus, keep going south, *there* you'll find gold.

Sailing down the Caribbean, Columbus began to hear of a much larger island ahead, a place called Colba (the Indian name) or Cuba. Surely this must be Cipango, he noted in his log. "There I will speak with the King and see if I can get the gold that I hear he wears."

Heading southwest, he reached Cuba on October 28, landing probably on the eastern side, now the Orient Province. When he came ashore, the beach was deserted, the few fishermen's huts empty of all but fishhooks, harpoons, and nets. The people had fled. Was this Japan? Where were the splendid palaces roofed in gold that he had long imagined? If the sad reality did not match his dreams, then the reality must be wrong.

Going by the geography he had invented, he convinced himself that Cuba was not an island but a continent—China. (Another large place nearby that the Indians spoke of must therefore be Japan.) He ordered a delegation led by de Torres to travel inland and find the emperor of China and hand him the letters of recommendation that Ferdinand and Isabella had given

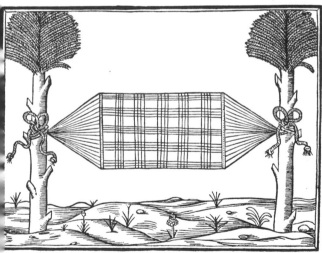

*European artists read descriptions of the early
voyages to America and drew their conceptions
of how things looked. A 1563 book depicts the
Indian method of navigation, and a 1547 book shows
an Indian hammock and the pineapple fruit.*

him for this purpose. (They were written in Latin). Moving up a valley the men saw many plants and birds, but the only "city" they found was a poor village of some fifty palm-thatched huts. De Torres was taken to the hut of the chief, the *cacique* of the region. His people, allowed to touch "men from the sky," then kneeled and kissed the hands and feet of the Spaniards. But the gold? No, the chief sighed, there is no gold in this village nor gold anywhere in this land. So the delegation turned back, bitterly disappointed.

On their way to the shore they came across a source of immense wealth—and grief—they could not recognize. They met men and women along the path "carrying torches of herbs whose smoke they drank, though it is impossible to see what sort of pleasure or profit they could have derived from it," says Las Casas. These "torches" the Indians called *tobacos*. The Indians sniffed the smoke a few times, then passed the burning herb to another. A hundred years later the craze for tobacco would begin to spread round the world.

Another hope unrealized. But Columbus would not quit. As the fleet sailed along the northern coast of this eastern end of Cuba, parties explored the shore on foot or went upstream in small boats. From one of these forays Martín Pinzón came back to report that natives had said that on an island to the east called Babeque the people gathered gold on the beach at night, and hammered it into rods. Columbus promptly ordered the caravels to seek out the fabulous place. One night, while out in the open sea, the *Pinta,* captained by Pinzón, disappeared. Had Pinzón, who had shown his impatience with the "reckless and heedless" command of Columbus, deliberately sailed away, deserting the fleet? Or was he lost in stormy seas?

The *Pinta* would be gone for nearly two months. It seems likely that the bold Pinzón had grown sick of the arrogance of the admiral, of his failure to confide in Pinzón, who felt superior in seamanship to this Genoese, this "foreign apprentice." So on his own, Pinzón scoured the seas for Babeque, and the gold and glory that would be his if he should be the first to find the treasure island. Columbus believed Pinzón had deserted him out of ''presumptuousness and greed''—sins the admiral was no less guilty of.

(The *Pinta* did come upon the island of Babeque—now called Great Inagua—but Pinzón found not a grain of gold there.)

10

"I Could Overrun All These Islands"

The fleet stayed in the harbor for several days. The ships were careened and their bottoms cleaned. Five young Indian men came aboard for a last visit, and in return for their trust, Columbus held them captive. He wanted to train them as interpreters, he said. Then he sent a boat ashore to kidnap seven women and three boys. Seeing this, the husbands and fathers of some of the victims begged to be taken along with them, rather than suffer the pain of separation. Columbus kindly agreed. A little later two of the young men escaped. The others? All would die before the fleet reached Spain.

Early in December, Columbus sighted what seemed to be a very large island the Indians called Bohio. It was Haiti. No Indians were visible; all had fled at the ships' approach. On December 12 Columbus raised a great cross on the northwest short of Haiti, taking possession in the name of Ferdinand and Isabella. He named the island Hispaniola in honor of Spain. (It now includes both Haiti and the Dominican Republic.) He sent a few men out to explore a valley near the harbor. They ran into a group of Indians, who fled, but they captured a beautiful young woman wearing a gold nose plug. Columbus decided to use her as a decoy, and giving her some castoff clothing and trinkets, he put her ashore.

A sketch of northwest Hispaniola,
drawn by Columbus.

The next day he sent several men with one of the captured Indians into the valley in the hope that the woman he let go the day before would have calmed her people's fears. The sailors came upon a large village of a thousand huts, but all the people fled as they neared it. When the Indian interpreter called out that these strange people were friends, not enemies, the villagers returned. The Spaniards were generously fed by them and given a flock of parrots as a gift. But there proved to be no gold there.

So the fleet sailed away again, this time stopping further east at Port de Paix. There some 500 people came down to the beach, led by a young chief. These were the Tainos of Haiti, an Arawak people Columbus found uncommonly handsome. He was excited to see so many gold ornaments worn by the villagers. It turned out that the young chief was subordinate to Guacanagari, the *cacique* who ruled over all northeastern Haiti.

Columbus treated the dignified chief with honor, but in his journal, meant to be read by Ferdinand and Isabella, he boasts how easy it will be to exploit these gentle Tainos. Even with so few Spaniards, he writes:

> I could overrun all these islands without opposition; for already I have seen but three of these mariners go ashore

where there was a multitude of these Indians, and all fled without their seeking to do them ill. They bear no arms, and are all unprotected and so very cowardly that a thousand would not face three; so they are fit to be ordered about and made to work, to sow and do aught else that may be needed, and you may build towns and teach them to go clothed and to adopt our customs.

Columbus could conceive no other connection between Spaniards and Indians than that between master and slave. He had already seen how the Portuguese had enslaved the natives in the Canaries and the blacks in Africa, and noted how the Church condoned it. Yet Las Casas, who would be the first priest ordained in the New World, took the words and example of Jesus deeply to heart, and in his biography of Columbus has this to say about the admiral's attitude:

Note here, that the natural, simple, and kind gentleness and humble condition of the Indians, and want of arms or protection, gave the Spaniards the insolence to hold them of little account, and to impose on them the harshest tasks that they could, and to become glutted with oppression and destruction. And sure it is that here the Admiral enlarged himself in speech more than he should, and that what he here conceived and set forth from his lips, was the beginning of the ill usage he afterwards inflicted upon them.

Sailing east, on December 20 Columbus anchored at Santo Tomás. The next day his men found a Taino village not far from the sea. The people gave the crew cassava bread and fruit and water. A day later came a messenger from Guacanagari, bearing the gift of a handsome cotton girdle embroidered with white and red fish bones, in whose center was a mask with the ears, tongue, and nose made of hammered gold.

The *cacique* was inviting Columbus to visit his village on the other side of Cape Haitien. The wary Columbus sent some men back with the messenger to see what his reception might be. While he waited, hundreds of Tainos came out to the *Santa María* in canoes, bearing gifts, including bits of gold. When the admiral asked where the gold had come from, he was told there was a rich gold-bearing region on the island.

On December 23 the boat returned from the *cacique*'s village, with baskets of gifts including pieces of gold, and the promise of warm hospitality. One of the *cacique*'s men spoke of a place in the center of the island he called Cibao—which Columbus immediately took to mean Cipango, or Japan—and said there was much gold there.

On Christmas Eve the *Santa María* and the *Niña* sailed out. Just as they were rounding the cape at midnight, on their way to Guacanagari, the *Santa María* grounded on a coral reef in the bay. Despite all the crew could do, the caravel was driven higher and higher on the reef by the swelling waves. The surge of the sea drove the ship down upon the rocks and the sharp coral punched holes in the wood. Rapidly the caravel filled with water. Nothing could be done to save her. Columbus and the crew ferried over to the *Niña* as his flagship went down.

They worked hard all Christmas day to try to float the *Santa María* and recover her stores, cargo, and equipment. Guacanagari responded to an appeal and sent all his canoes and men to help salvage what they could. The next day the *cacique* came aboard the *Niña* to comfort the weeping admiral, saying that "he must not show grief, that he would give him all he had, and that he had given the Christians who were ashore two very big houses, and would give more if necessary." "To such an extent are they loyal and without greed for the property of others," noted Columbus in his journal.

Columbus had the *cacique* he admired so much dine with him aboard the *Niña,* and in turn, on shore, the *cacique* gave Columbus a dinner of lobster and yams and cassava bread. As they talked through interpreters, Guacanagari told Columbus of another Indian group, the Caribs. These were a warlike set of cannibals from the South American coasts who gave their name to the Caribbean Sea and added the word "cannibal" to the English language. On their invasions of the islands of the Caribbean they fought fiercely with bows and arrows and terrified such gentle people as the Tainos. Columbus assured Guacanagari that Spaniards had the military power to overcome the Caribs, and displayed not only his Turkish-made bows and arrows but fired off muskets—weapons the Indians had never seen or heard of. It reassured the *cacique* that he had a true friend in this white man.

To Columbus, the shipwreck was no disaster, but God's gift. God had willed it, he believed, so that the admiral could discover the gold of Cibao. If the ship had not gone down he would have missed this place. He would take advantage of his luck by founding a colony here. Such a settlement had not been his original intent on this voyage, for he had taken along only enough men to crew his fleet. But with the *Pinta* still missing, and the *Santa María* sunk, the little *Niña* could not contain her own crew of forty plus the *Santa María*'s twenty-two men.

He gave orders to build a settlement on the shore of the bay, and called it La Navidad. Note how he gives pious Christian names to all the places he visits. It was natural for a man who believed it his divinely appointed mission to plant the True Faith among the world's pagans. This was the first attempt at European colonization in the New World. Using the timbers of the *Santa María* the men made a fort and in its cellar stored seeds for crops and trinkets to trade for the gold of Cibao they could almost feel in their hands. The admiral selected thirty-nine men from the two caravels, and in command of the settlement placed Diego de Harana, the fleet's marshal. The men chosen to stay felt themselves the lucky ones. They held a small boat saved from the flagship, so they could explore the region and find the gold mine.

*The 1493 edition of the Columbus letter
shows the fort built at Navidad.*

On January 4, 1493, Columbus set sail for Spain. He hoped to arrive before Pinzón could get there and announce the discovery of the Indies. But two days later the *Niña* spied the *Pinta* sailing toward them. The captain came aboard the admiral's caravel. Pinzón said he had reached the territory of another *cacique,* Caonabo, and had found much gold there. While lying in harbor, he had heard of the shipwreck and was sailing to offer help when he encountered the *Niña.*

Columbus suspected this was not the whole truth but was glad to have the *Pinta* along on the voyage home. He was angry to learn that Pinzón had kept for himself half the gold he had found, and was carrying six Indians he had kidnapped. Although the admiral himself was guilty of the same, he had these Indians put ashore.

They spent a few more days preparing for the Atlantic passage. Then on January 8 they set sail along northern Hispaniola. At one point they anchored on Samana Bay so that the crew could go ashore to pick up yams needed for their larder. On the beach they were met by a band of Ciguayos, Arawaks who carried bows and arrows, weapons the Spaniards had never before seen in the islands. At some misperceived threat, the Spaniards slashed one Indian with a sword and wounded another with an arrow. The Indians fled, but Columbus was uneasy at this first sign of danger and decided to leave the bay. On January 16 the *Pinta* and the *Niña* began the first homeward voyage from the New World to the Old.

11

Admiral of
the Ocean Sea

When Columbus set off for Spain from Hispaniola he was once again trying to accomplish what no one before him had ever done. Centuries later, sailing east to Europe across the Atlantic would be a routine voyage. The way was sure and safe. But in 1493, Columbus was the first to attempt it. He could not follow the path of his outward journey. That would mean heading into the trade winds that had carried him west. So he decided to bear north, hoping to find a zone of favorable winds that would carry him toward Spain.

As it turned out, he was unable to steer straight east-northeast, but had to tack many times in several directions. When the ships reached the latitude of the Bermudas, they found westerly winds that blew them toward Spain. By this happy accident he pioneered the route ships would routinely take from North America to Europe.

Sailing on the mid-Atlantic the *Niña* and the *Pinta* made a hundred miles (160 km) a day. With the sea calm, the crews looked ahead eagerly to a great welcome home. About three weeks out, the sky turned bleak, the rains came down, the air grew chill. Winter. Now they were entering a turbulent part of the Atlantic, where air fronts collided to create violent storms. They ran head on into the worst blow any of them had ever seen. The crews feared the ships might go down. Columbus ordered the caravels to lie to, with sails shortened, making no attempt to follow a course. They went where the winds drove them. The first night of the storm the *Pinta* disappeared into the dark. The *Niña*'s crew, terrified, prayed constantly to the Lord for help and vowed to make pilgrimages to holy shrines if only they would survive.

But for the next two days and nights the hurricane blew ever wilder; every soul aboard felt doomed—even Columbus, who was so supremely confident that he was doing the Lord's own work and would not be abandoned. Would his great achievement in discovering the westward route to the Indies never be known if the ships sank? Quickly he wrote down on parchment a brief report of the voyage, wrapped it in oilskin, placed it in a barrel, and tossed it overboard. (It never turned up.)

At the end of the storm's third day, the wind shifted and the waves lost their terrible force. At sunrise on February 15, land was sighted; it proved to be Santa Maria, the southernmost island of the Azores. Portuguese territory! Columbus had no desire to stop there, but he had no choice. He needed to give his men rest, and take on water and wood and food. After four days at sea without rest, he managed to sleep. His legs were numb from exposure to cold and wet. He would never recover from the arthritis that began to trouble him now.

The *Niña* dropped anchor at a coastal village, astonishing the local fishermen, who believed no ship could have outsailed the storm that had just ended. Some of the crew went ashore to offer thanks in a chapel of the Virgin Mary, while Columbus kept the rest on board. As the men prayed, they were taken prisoner by the island's governor. He thought these Spaniards were trading illegally in Portuguese waters. When they replied they had just sailed in from the Indies, no one would believe them.

Columbus demanded that the governor free his men and, when he refused, threatened to capture 100 of the islanders and take them to Spain as slaves. The governor relented when he examined Columbus's papers and saw that he was truly on an official Spanish mission.

On February 24 the *Niña* set off again and headed for the Spanish port of Palos, a week's voyage away. But the ship ran into another violent storm not far off Portugal's coast, and Columbus had to sail up the Tagus and anchor off Lisbon. The date was March 4, 1493.

While lying offshore the Azores, Columbus wrote a report of this first voyage. He did it in the form of a letter to Santangel, the crown official who had persuaded Ferdinand and Isabella to back the Enterprise of the Indies. Of course it was meant for Their Majesties' eyes. He planned to send it to the court as soon as he arrived in Palos, and he did. It would be his announcement to the world of what he had accomplished. His journal he kept with him to present to the king and queen himself. The letter, written in Spanish, was quickly printed in pamphlet form in several editions in Spanish, Latin, and Italian.

Most of the facts he reported have already been given here. He thought he had discovered the westward passage to Asia, and that was what he wrote he had done. He wanted the crown and everyone else to believe he had accomplished what he had promised. It was in his own interest to convince the world of the success of his epochal voyage. His letter never mentions failures or disasters, not the sinking of the *Santa María,* not the troubles with Martín Pinzón, not the rebelliousness of the sailors. (He does not tell what course he took nor what distances he covered, for that would have given crucial information to competitive nations.) He did not claim to have seen the Great Khan of China or the riches of Cipango, but he built up a case for their being just over the horizon, so close he would reach them on the next voyage.

He made no claim to having found new lands no European had ever seen. No, he wanted these Caribbean islands to be the Asian countries Marco Polo had described, with fantastic treasure just for the taking. So he begins his letter by saying, "As I know that you will be happy with the great success with which the Lord has crowned my voyage, I write to tell you that I crossed in thirty-three days from the Canaries to the Indies. . . . I found very many islands and took possession of them all. No opposition was offered. . . ." And as he goes on to describe the places he visited he adds that of the many rivers he saw, "the majority contain gold. . . . There are many spices, and great mines of gold and other metals. . . ." This was fantasy, not reality.

After telling how peaceful and generous the Indians were, he says: "I gave them a thousand pretty things in order to get their affection and make them want to become Christians. I hope to win them to the love and service of your Highnesses and of the Spanish nation, and make them collect and give us the things which they possess in abundance and which we need."

Coming to his landing at Hispaniola he describes the tiny cluster of huts as "a large town" and Guacanagari as "king of the land" with whom he "established a warm friendship. But should he change his attitude the men I have left [at Navidad] would be enough to destroy the entire country."

Holding out the promise of much more, he notes that this was only "a very hasty voyage." If their majesties would give him a little more help, "I will give them as much gold as they need . . . spices . . . cotton . . . resin . . . aloes . . . and as many slaves as they ask." Again, all this, except for the slaves, was what he *wished* he had found, not what he actually found.

He reminds his readers that there were some who didn't believe he could do all this, but he *had* done it, for "thus the eternal God, Our Lord, gives victory to those who follow His way over apparent impossibilities."

He dates the letter February 15, 1493, and signs it "The Admiral"—a reminder of a promise made to him.

Lisbon was the last place Columbus wanted to land. After his troubles at the Azores he decided to prepare a letter to King John of Portugal asking permission to sail up the Tagus to Lisbon, where he hoped to have the storm's damage to the *Niña* repaired. When the warship standing guard at the channel challenged him, he showed his Spanish papers, and announced that he had just come back from the Indies.

The news caused a great sensation; the people flocked to the wharves to see the caravel and the Indians it carried. King John sent word he wanted Columbus to pay him a call. The admiral was not eager for a meeting with the monarch who had turned him down years before. Still, he could not refuse (and this would give him a chance to gloat a little). The king cleared the way for him to sail up the Tagus to Lisbon, and extended credit at the royal shipyards for the repair of the *Niña*.

Because the plague was sweeping Lisbon, the king had Columbus meet him in a monastery outside the city. The admiral came under royal escort, accompanied by the healthiest of the ten captive Indians who had survived the voyage. John listened skeptically to the strange story, unable to believe it was really the Indies this rejected petitioner had reached, and suspecting it might rather have been some outlying territory of the Azores, belonging to Portugal.

King John did not want Portugal's monopoly of trade with West Africa nor her hoped-for monopoly of the best route to India to be endangered. You know, he said, that under a treaty with Spain that my father signed in 1479, the lands you visited belong to Portugal. Columbus replied that he knew nothing of that treaty, but he could assure the king he had not sailed to Africa, but to the Indies. The rather arrogant tone he adopted infuriated John's listening courtiers. They urged the king to execute "that braggart." But unwilling to offend Spain, the king let him return to Lisbon, where he found the *Niña* fitted out with new sails and ready to leave.

On March 15—thirty-two weeks after sailing from Palos—the *Niña* dropped anchor in its old port, only to find that the missing *Pinta* had come in just before it. Pinzón had landed earlier at another Spanish port and had sent word to Their Majesties in Barcelona of the success of the mission. But he was told not to appear at court without Columbus. Sick from the hardships of the voyage, and never happy in his troubled relationship with Columbus, Pinzón was bitterly disappointed. He quit his ship in Palos and took to his bed. Within a few weeks he was dead.

The people of Palos crowded aboard the *Niña* and the *Pinta,* eager to hear tales of the great adventure and to see the strange people of the Indies. Columbus sent a messenger on the 800-mile (1,300-km) ride to Barcelona, where the sovereigns were holding court. In three weeks came their reply: Columbus was to come at once to court. The message was addressed to "Don Cristobal Colon, their Admiral of the Ocean Sea and Governor of the Islands that he hath discovered in the Indies." So quickly was his achievement recognized and the rewards promised him confirmed.

The sovereigns' letter urged him to begin preparations at once for another voyage to the Indies. They believed what he said he had done. He had found the way to the Indies by taking a westward shortcut. Success, yes, but costly. To make it pay off, it must be followed up, and quickly, before other powers could push their way in.

Columbus promptly wrote out a plan for colonization of Hispaniola. He wanted to recruit up to 2,000 voluntary settlers, and with them to build three or four towns, each with its own corps of administrators, and enough priests and friars to convert the Indians and teach them the Lord's ways. He recognized that greed for gold, not any Christianizing mission, would be the only lure to draw settlers to Hispaniola. To control what he foresaw as a mad drive to get rich quick, he proposed regulations for gold hunting and for trade between the colony and the mother country.

This letter by a messenger hurried ahead while Columbus traveled at the more stately pace befitting his new high rank. He was accompanied by officers, servants, and six Indians, who carried brilliantly colored parrots in cages and wore their gold ornaments. Along the road to Barcelona crowds came to stare at the admiral and his heathen captives. At Cordova he paused to see his two sons, Diego and Ferdinand, and some old friends. In mid-April he reached Barcelona, where "all the court and city came out" to greet the Admiral of the Ocean Sea.

Now was the time to revel in all the honors Columbus had dreamed should be his. At the Alcazar the king and queen received him with great pomp. They rose from their thrones when he approached, and when he kneeled to kiss their hands they asked him to rise and sit beside them, with his hat on, a very rare privilege. Their Majesties looked over the many strange things he had brought home and studied the Indians closely. After questioning him at length about the newfound islands they talked of plans for the next voyage. In the royal chapel they all gave thanks to Heaven for the marvelous discoveries.

Columbus remained several weeks in Barcelona as a royal guest, meeting grandees, enjoying sumptuous dinners, elaborating plans for his second voyage. The six Indians were baptized, with Isabella and her son as godparents. One of the Indians would stay in Spain, but die in two years. The five others would start back to Hispaniola with Columbus, but three of them didn't live to see home again. The sovereigns made Columbus a nobleman, conferring on him and his descendants the right to a coat of arms, which he blazoned on the banners of all the ships he would command. They also gave his two brothers, Bartholomew and Diego, the privilege of being called "Don." All the other rights and privileges in his original agreement with the crown were reconfirmed as well. It meant he had full jurisdic-

*Columbus traveling through Spain on his way
to meet Their Majesties at Barcelona. Behind him
are his Indian captives, and chained to a
platform are birds and animals from the islands.
A fanciful drawing made long after the event.*

When made a nobleman by the Spanish rulers,
Columbus was given the right to this coat of arms.

tion over his discoveries and the Spanish ships sailing to and from the Indies.

To make sure of the crown's title to Columbus's discoveries, Ferdinand and Isabella began negotiations with Portugal and the Vatican. They looked to Columbus for information and advice in this difficult diplomacy.

Sitting on the throne of St. Peter was His Holiness Alexander VI; he had been elected pope in 1492. It was now up to him to clear up who the newly discovered islands belonged to. Were they King John's, as the ruler of Portugal claimed? Or were

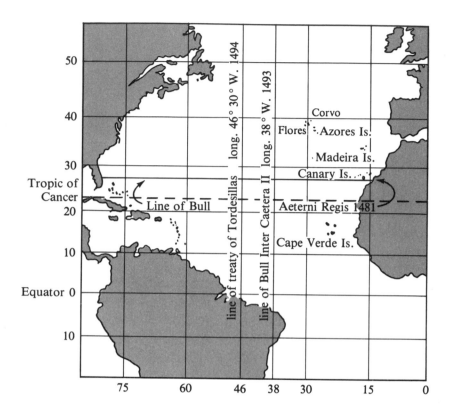

*The lines of demarcation drawn
between Spanish and Portuguese
territories by Pope Alexander VI*

they Spain's? What other nations might think did not matter to the two countries. They appealed to the pope to settle how the world should be divided between them. The Church maintained that all newly found lands not ruled by a Christian monarch "belonged" to the pope. His was the power to hand such lands as fiefs to whatever kings he chose, who would then be obliged to convert the pagan peoples to the True Faith. (It seems no one wondered what the rulers of Japan or China might think of this division of their countries.)

The pope, a Spaniard of the Borgia family whom the historian Daniel Boorstin describes as "notoriously dissolute," was heavily indebted to Ferdinand and Isabella and glad to do their bidding. He agreed that they should be granted "all they had conquered so far and also everything they would still discover farther west as far as the Orient, and forbade all others to encroach on these boundaries." In May 1493 he set a demarcation line running from the North to the South Pole about 400 land miles (650 km) west of the Azores; everything west of that line would go to Spain. Portugal did not like this; John wanted to push the region of Spanish exploration as far west as possible, to rule Spain out of any possible southward route across the central Atlantic. He was successful in this, for in 1494 when the two powers began direct negotiations in the Spanish town of Tordesillas, they reached agreement to move the line about 1,400 miles (2,250 km) west of the Cape Verde Islands. Thus the Treaty of Tordesillas prevented any Spanish interference on this route to India, and, as it turned out, gave Brazil to Portugal. A line of demarcation was later applied also to the Pacific, roughly dividing the whole overseas world into Spanish and Portuguese zones of exploration.

Left out in the cold, the other European powers were unhappy with this outcome, and later would flout it. Spain, however, got the bigger slice of the western hemispheric pie, and did everything it could to hang on to it. When foreign sailors were caught in Spain's half of the world, they were murdered. And the Native Americans, whose homelands were so easily claimed by a foreign power? They had nothing to say about the loss of their freedom and independence. Presumably they should be thankful to come to Christ under the benevolent protection of European monarchs.

12

The Second Voyage

The news moved through Europe as printers quickly published in pamphlet or newsletter form the letter of Columbus summarizing his voyage. Within a year there were twelve editions. It was a striking illustration of the role of printing in spreading new information and ideas. The various editions roused great interest wherever they circulated. It was the first major voyage of discovery to be reported to the world in the commander's own words, with his interpretation of its geographical significance.

How did Europe react to the news? Spain, of course, enthusiastically accepted Columbus's claims. The Portuguese said nothing. They believed Columbus had come across a group of worthless islands out in the Atlantic. So long as the Spanish stayed away from Portuguese territory, King John didn't care. The news traveled slowly to northern Europe, where it caused little fuss.

In Italy, however, long the European crossroads for commercial travels, there was wide commentary on the news. Diplomats, businessmen, scientists, writers gossiped in their letters about the discovery and its meaning. They were excited about the promise of new sources of gold, about the curious appearance and customs of the island natives, about the exotic plants and animals.

Occanica Classis

De Insulis inuentis

Epistola Cristoferi Colom (cui etas nostra
multũ debet : de Insulis in mari Indico nup
inuẽtis. Ad quas perquirendas octauo antea
mense: auspicijs et ere Inuictissimi Fernandi
Ibispaniarum Regis missus fuerat) ad Mag=
nificum dñm Raphaelez Sanzis: eiusdẽ sere=
nissimi Regis Thesaurariũ missa. quam nobi
lis ac litterat⁹ vir Aliander 8 Cosco: ab Ibis=
pano ydeomate in latinũ conuertit: tercio kls
Maij. M.cccc.xciij. Pontificatus Alexandri
Sexti Anno Primo .

Uoniam suscepte prouintie rem p=
fectam me psecutum fuisse: gratũ ti
bi fore scio: bas pstitui crarare: que
te vniuscuiuscq rei in hoc nostro iti=
nere geste inuentecq admoneãt. Tricesimoter
tio die postcq Sadibus discessi: in mare Indi=
cũ perueni: vbi plurimas Insulas innumeris
habitatas hominib⁹ repperi: quaꝛ oim p feli=
cissimo Rege nostro: preconio celebrato ꞇ ve=
rillis extensis cõtradicente nemine possessio=
nẽ accepi. primecq earum: diui Saluatoꝛis no
men imposui (cuius fret⁹ aurilio) tam ad bãc
cq ad ceteras alias puenim⁹. Eam vero Indi

j

First page of the Columbus letter reporting his
voyage. Opposite: a woodcut of the Santa Maria.

Not many tried to pin down precisely where these new islands might be. Businessmen who had funds to invest wondered if Columbus's islands would be profitable. Suppose the Portuguese were right, and the islands were nowhere near Asia? Or if Columbus was right, and the islands were part of Asia, were they just remote and primitive places of no commercial value?

Columbus himself did not claim he had discovered a new world. No, he would go down to his grave insisting he had found a new route to the old world of Asia. But soon after his letter appeared, one man began to speak of him as "this famous Columbus, discoverer of a New World." The writer was Peter Martyr, of Italian birth but for many years living at the Spanish court. He was chaplain to Isabella, humanist, diplomat, and purveyor of news by letter to many important people in Europe. He was there in Barcelona to see Columbus arrive in April 1493. Always eager to get the personal reports of explorers, he patched together what he learned in a book called *The New World*. Peter Martyr was not an uncritical reporter. His book indicates he wanted to believe Columbus, only there was the nagging question of the way the admiral had tailored Ptolemy's ancient geography to fit his own interests. Still, he gave Columbus the benefit of the doubt. It should be understood that by "the new world" Martyr and others who began to use the same term meant not the western hemisphere, but those scattered islands on the Atlantic, the outermost extension of Asia, unknown to Europeans before Columbus.

The 1493 letter reporting Columbus's voyage was the first of many narratives of exploration to appear. But only those people directly involved with overseas trade or the planning of voyages of discovery were deeply interested. Not until the middle of the next century would such narratives win a broader readership.

Some speculated that if Columbus was right and had reached Asia by sailing west just thirty-three days from the Canaries, then Ptolemy was wrong. That conclusion was a hard one for any scholar to accept. It was only when Ferdinand Magellan, sailing in 1519 on what proved to be the longest voyage of all, completed his circumnavigation of the globe in 1521 that Ptolemy was seen to be right and Columbus wrong about the extent of the globe.

But when the second voyage of Columbus was about to begin, everyone thought he would reach those Asian lands Marco Polo had described. Surely the richer Indies were just a bit beyond his first findings. No one knew he had stood on the doorstep of a vast new continent. Columbus least of all. To the end of his life, says his biographer Samuel Eliot Morison, he "remained stubbornly and obstinately, absolutely and completely wrong."

Only five months after returning to Spain, Columbus was ready to set forth again. The aim of the first voyage had been exploratory. Now he must make his discoveries pay off. He had no difficulty in raising volunteers for the voyage. His now famous letter was like a sales promotion piece, whipping up the appetite for gold and glory. To organize the expedition the crown assigned Juan de Fonseca, archdeacon of Seville, who would act as quartermaster general for this and the other voyages to come. He was an unimaginative bureaucrat, mean and tightfisted, whose authority Columbus would repeatedly question and sometimes defy. It made for the arrogant admiral still another enemy at a court which already numbered many who disliked him.

The flagship Columbus chose he named the *Santa María,* honoring the first, sunken vessel. The *Niña* went along too, with some of its crew drawn again from the Niño family who owned her. But no Pinzóns: that family had had enough of the admiral. This time Columbus commanded a large fleet—seventeen ships with some 1,200 people (no women among them). They included his crews and artisans, farmers, gentleman-soldiers seeking their fortune, six priests to convert the heathen, and various officials to keep the books and enforce order. Aboard too was

Dr. Diego Chanca, a court physician who would make a report of the voyage. (No log kept by Columbus for this voyage has come down to us.) None of the ships were heavily armed. They carried no trading goods, only the usual trinkets to barter with natives.

The fleet's mission was to build a permanent colony on Hispaniola. Columbus had said there was much gold to be found there, and that the soil was fertile for farming. The ships carried enough food to sustain the colonizers for some months, until they could live off the crops they would raise themselves. To that end the fleet stowed away grain seeds and cereals, grapevines, and a variety of animals for breeding, such as horses, pigs, and sheep. To prepare so large an expedition in such short time was a remarkable feat for fifteenth-century Spain.

Plans called for alloting periods of time to hunt for gold, and periods for farming. Eager for acquiring riches himself, Columbus knew that greed could drive out all other considerations. This was to be Spain's first planting of a colony in a new land, and he, like the crown, wanted it to endure. With Columbus began the wave of emigration from one continent to another that would never end.

On September 25, 1493, the fleet left Cádiz, 60 miles (97 km) down the coast from Palos. The Canaries were once again the first port of call. They left those islands on October 13, and three weeks later, on November 3, made landfall on Dominica, a wild Carib island. This time the passage had been easy. Easy, despite Columbus's elementary knowledge of navigation. That he could return to lands he had first come upon by sheer chance was remarkable. Remember that he had few or none of the instruments for celestial navigation; he depended upon his practical skill at dead reckoning. It was enough to get him from one known location to another.

From Dominica the fleet sailed north along the superb arc of the Lesser Antilles. At Guadeloupe some men went ashore "for purposes of plunder," said Michele de Cuneo, an old friend of the admiral who left an account of this voyage. When the party failed to return, search groups went out who found deserted Carib huts and gruesome evidence of cannibalism. The Spaniards captured some of the Caribs in the woods. They noted that their prisoners were dark-skinned and painted their bodies red. Their hair was shaven clean on one side of the head, and streamed down in long braids on the other side. Even aboard ship they struggled "like lions in chains."

Although they found no gold, the Spaniards tasted pineapple for the first time. Four days later the lost crewmen showed up. To the Carib captives the fleet added twelve "very beautiful and plump" teenage Arawak girls.

It was mid-November now, but the tropical air and water were still very warm. The fleet lay to at what is now St. Croix in the Virgins, populated by Caribs. Here Columbus had his first bloody encounter with Indians. A party went ashore to take on fresh water, moved inland, and came to a village most of whose people had just fled. The Spaniards captured some Arawak boys and girls who had been enslaved by the Caribs.

As their boat was returning to the fleet, a Carib canoe paddled round the point and stopped abruptly, stunned by the sight of the vast Spanish fleet anchored in the harbor. For a long hour the four men, two women, and a boy aboard the canoe stayed motionless on the water, staring in wonder at the huge ships and the white men gazing at them from the decks. The shore party meanwhile maneuvered their boat so as to cut off the Caribs' escape. Seeing that flight was impossible, the Indians shot arrows at the Spaniards, wounding one and killing another. But they were soon overpowered and taken to the fleet. One of the men, whose belly was sliced by a Spaniard's sword, was tossed overboard. He did not sink, but clutching his guts with one hand, swam with the other toward shore. The Spaniards chased after him, pulled him aboard, tied his hands and feet, and threw him back into the sea. The Indian managed to free himself, and again swam off. Then the gallant whites, frustrated in their repeated

*When reports of cannibals encountered by
Columbus reached Europe, artists began
to make gruesome images of their practices,
as in this engraving of 1621.*

attempts at murder, shot the Indian through and through with arrows until he died.

While the great courage of the Indians did not win mercy, it deeply impressed the militaristic Spaniards. They soon found the Carib women were just as brave. Cuneo tells how he tried to rape one he had made his slave. She fought back so violently he had to whip her with a rope before he could subdue her. That evening, he joined all the other Spaniards in singing a hymn to the Blessed Virgin.

Sailing away, the fleet reached the large island we call Puerto Rico, but which its people called Borinquen. Columbus kept to the southern coast, staying clear of the reefs until he came to a bay with good anchorage, and took on water. This was the last major island the fleet would discover on its outward voyage.

Now, as they steered for Hispaniola, the two Arawak guides—the only survivors of the many captives taken on the first voyage—began to recognize their homeland. Columbus put one ashore, hoping the man would convince his people that Christians were friendly folk. The fleet sailed along the northern coast until two days later a shore party found dreadful evidence of the fate of the men stationed in the Navidad garrison almost a year ago. Four dead Spaniards lay on a riverbank, their rotting remains fastened with rope.

Columbus was alarmed by the news. As evening came on, he hurried the ships toward Navidad, sending up flares and firing a cannon so that the garrison would know of his coming. But only silence from the shore. Fearing to enter Navidad in the dark, Columbus decided to wait until morning. As the fleet lay to, a canoe approached the flagship, with messengers sent by Guacanagari. They brought gifts of golden masks and told the admiral all was well. Their chief had not come because he had been wounded in a fight with a rival *cacique,* Caonabo. Their nervous manner was suspicious; the captive Indian interpreter pressed them hard, and found that all the garrison were dead.

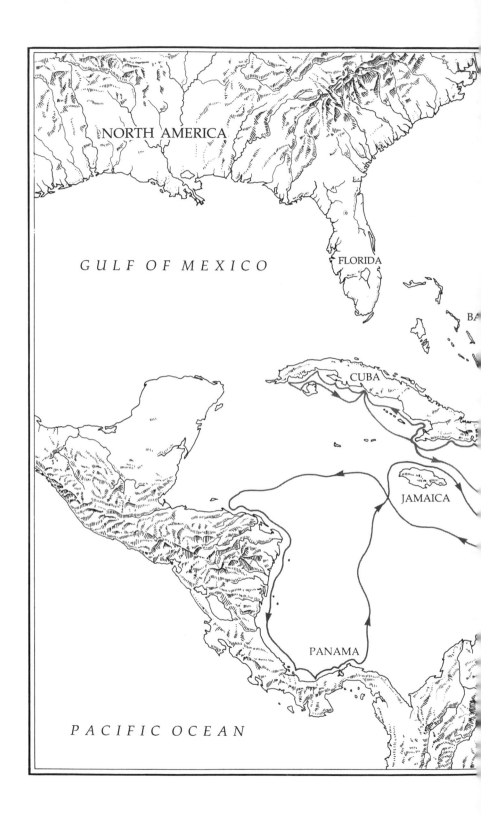

NORTH AMERICA

GULF OF MEXICO

FLORIDA

BA

CUBA

JAMAICA

PANAMA

PACIFIC OCEAN

Columbus in the Americas

N

0   500 Miles

Voyage 1
1492-1493

ATLANTIC OCEAN

Voyage 2
1493-1494

Voyage 4
1502-1503

Voyage 3
1498

ANIOLA
DOMINICAN
REPUBLIC

PUERTO RICO

SEA

SOUTH AMERICA

Columbus refused to believe it. How could such "gentle, timid souls" destroy his tough Spaniards?

When dawn came, the crews rushed to the shore. The fort they had built from the wreckage of the *Santa María* had been razed to the ground. The corpses of the men left behind—all forty of them—were found scattered around the ashes, or miles off, killed while trying to escape.

In a few days Columbus learned from Guacanagari and other Indians the truth of what had happened at Navidad. No sooner had Columbus left the fort to sail home, then the colonists began quarreling and fighting. Everyone was out for himself. Any sense of a common effort to build a lasting community disappeared. None would take orders from others. Discipline did not exist. Two forces shattered the colony: the lust for gold and the lust for women. Bands of Spanish thieves roved the countryside, plundered the villages, forced Indians to hunt for gold. Any girl or woman the Spaniards fancied was taken prisoner and made a sex slave.

Guacanagari was unable to defend his people from the predatory Spaniards. But when the brutal gangs moved onto the territory of Caonabo, they met fierce resistance. He captured one gang leader and executed him on the spot. Then he led a strong force of his men to Navidad where they found only ten settlers who had stayed in the fort. He killed them all. And every Spaniard hiding out in the woods, he flushed out and killed.

Guacanagari had tried to save some lives, but Caonabo's men would not let him stand in their way. The "people from Heaven" who had roused wonderment and awe when their ships sailed into the quiet harbors of the New World had quickly shown how cruel and uncivilized the white man could be. And by demonstrating how fiercely they would defend their independence, the Indians had shattered the image of the passive "good savage."

But Columbus did not pause for regret. He still thought first of gold. Before he had returned to Spain he had ordered the colonists to bury all the gold they might find. Now he had his men dig under the ruins of Navidad for the gold. They found only rags and garbage. After a quick funeral service he led the fleet away in search of a site for a new colony. He seemed strangely indifferent to the terrible deeds he had learned of, and to what they signified. His way out of trouble was to run away from it. His imagination had created a dream world in the Indies, and when reality intruded, he chased after the next dream.

The precise location of Navidad had long been sought. In the opinion of archeologists from the University of Florida, it is probably what is now called En Bas Saline.

The new site Columbus chose was east of Navidad on the north coast of Hispaniola. It was a wooded peninsula with a good harbor, not far, he thought, from the gold mines he believed to be nearby in the interior. He named the new town Isabela, after his patron queen. The site was badly chosen, for the coastal region was marshy and unhealthy. He sent a squad inland to scout for the gold deposits. When the men spotted a few traces of gold in mountain streams they rushed back elated with the news. But before Columbus could follow up, heavy rains flooded the town and several hundred men fell sick—not only from the damp but from tropical heat, the changed diet, the hard labor of building a town, and the swarms of insects infesting the swamps. No doubt many of the men were dispirited by the gross contrast between this harsh reality and the idyllic picture Columbus had drawn in his report on the first voyage.

By the end of January Columbus decided he needed still more help, and sent twelve of the smaller ships back to Spain with a message to Ferdinand and Isabella asking for a few more caravels with fresh food, medicines for the sick, more clothing, mules, and a hundred experienced miners to carry on prospecting for gold.

Meanwhile Columbus himself led an expedition into the mountains to build a fort close by the mining region. So beautiful was the valley he saw beyond the first mountain range that he thought he had come to "a corner of paradise." By a river, he started a crew of fifty men to work on the fort, which he called Santo Tomás. Hard as they hunted, the only gold to be found was a few chips and grains. Could this be the Cipango Marco Polo had described, so rich in gold that palace roofs were made of the precious metal? And Asia itself: where was that continent?

Leaving the fort builders and miners, he went back to the town of Isabela. Now the sick were dying, and defeatism poisoned the air. Let's go back to Spain, the colonists clamored; there is nothing here for us. Columbus kept silent, trusting no one, confiding in no one. Rumors began of another surge of Indian protest. A few of them had stolen from Spaniards after Spaniards had stolen from them. Ignoring his guilty men, Columbus had the hands of the accused Indians cut off. Tension built; mutiny threatened. But instead of acting to restore discipline and build morale, Columbus chose to leave Isabela. Proof, proof that he had indeed reached the Indies was what he desperately desired. The urge to resume the search for the mainland of Asia overwhelmed all else in his fevered imagination. He would leave his troubles behind, in the care of his brother Diego, and sail off "to explore the world of the Indies," as he put it.

Late in April 1494, he started out with three caravels, heading for Cuba. He had convinced himself that this was truly the mainland he had promised to find. As the fleet sailed away, the admiral sniffed "the delicate aromas of flowers spread across the sea." He had already seen some of Cuba's northern coast, so he tried the southern coast this time. Reaching Cape Cruz he asked the Indians on the shore where he would find gold. On an island nearby, they replied, pointing south to Jamaica. But a week of roaming that island's shores turned up no sign of gold. The Indians on this island were not friendly like the Arawaks. To teach them a lesson, Columbus's crossbowmen killed some of them and turned loose the trained dogs brought from Spain to savage the unarmed and naked men and women.

Back to Cuba, winding in and out of the maze of islands nearby. When the crews were not worrying about running aground on shoals and reefs they were battling with storms. All this trouble and danger, and for what? Their provisions were almost gone, their bodies exhausted, their spirits low. Let's go back, they urged the admiral.

Columbus said nothing. What assurance of a profitable voyage could he offer them? Did he know himself what he was after? Only one thing—proof that he had reached the Indies. After all his searching, this *must* be it, this Cuba *must* be mainland Asia.

He did a strange thing to prove it. On June 12, 1494, when the ships were some hundred miles (160 km) away from the southwestern tip of Cuba, he called in his fleet secretary, Fernando Perez de Luna, the man who was also Isabella's public notary. He ordered him to go aboard all three of the caravels and question every pilot, officer, and seaman "if they had any doubt as to whether this land was the continent of the Indies." Each man questioned was to voice his own opinion, to be recorded by the notary. Men who had no doubts would then take an oath, saying that they had reached Asia, and that this was their own opinion. The oath, once recorded, could not be withdrawn. Any man who violated that oath would be punished by a huge fine or having his tongue cut out.

He was convinced this was not an island, but part of the Malay archipelago, a peninsula. Why go further? Some think this forcing of an oath was a sign of madness. His stubborn belief in himself, and the power of his imagination to remake reality, drove him to the coercion of his crew. And had not Bartholomew Diaz extracted such an oath from his seamen? It had happened in 1488: Diaz had rounded the Cape of Good Hope and was sailing to India when his crew refused to go any

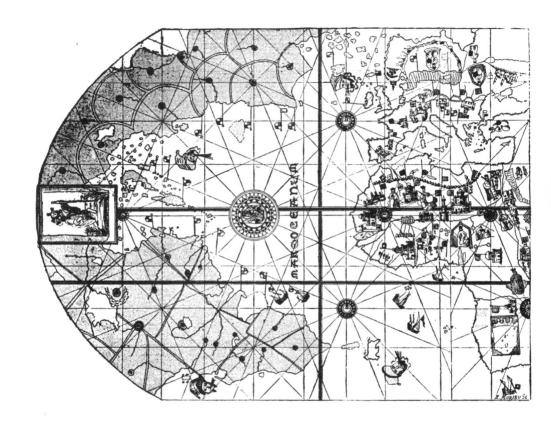

The earliest world chart to depict both
the Old and New worlds. It was drawn by
Juan de la Cosa, cartographer who sailed
with Columbus. On the left are the Caribbean
islands and the northeast coast of South
America. To the right are Europe and Africa.

further. Diaz was forced to return to Lisbon, but first he had each man sign a document saying that Africa had indeed been rounded and the way east to the Indies found.

None of Columbus's men refused to sign the oath. They must have felt they had to if they were ever to return home alive. Besides, like Columbus, their experience told them no island could be as long as Cuba was. One who signed the oath was Juan de la Cosa, a cartographer and pilot aboard the *Niña*. Around 1500 he would draw the earliest world chart to include both the Old and the New Worlds. He must have changed his mind about Cuba, for in this chart he shows it as an island, though it is unclear whether it represents part of Asia, or part of a separate continent.

Ironically, if Columbus had only sailed that hundred miles further west, he would have seen that Cuba really was an island and not a continent. And he might have heard from the Indians something about Yucatan and Mexico, which were so close by and *were* part of the great continent of America. In Mexico too was all the wealth his voyages would never turn up.

13

Gold Hunts
and Manhunts

On June 13, the day after the oath of Cuba, Columbus directed the fleet back to Isabela. The return was rough, made worse by the admiral's sickness. He "fell into a pestilential sleep that robbed him of all his faculties and strength," wrote Las Casas, "so that he seemed as though dead. Everyone thought that he would not live another day." The fleet sailed among cays and shoals, with the *Niña* once running aground. They sighted great flocks of crows or cormorants and plowed through acres of turtles, which the men collected by the boatload and boiled for the meat. Huge oysters were picked up; though no pearls were found in them, they tasted good.

It was slow going against the winds. It took twenty-five days to make just 200 miles (320 km). Then came worse weather—thunderous squalls and the danger of drowning. They stopped now and then at islands where friendly Indians gave them gifts of food. Once, anchored for a night at a Jamaican bay, the *cacique* of a nearby village came out with three canoes to visit. How the Indians appeared to Columbus is described by Andrés Bernaldez, a Spanish curate with whom Columbus stayed for a while on his return from this second voyage, and to whom he told his adventures:

> In the largest canoe he came in person with his wife and
> two daughters, one of whom was about eighteen years

old, very beautiful, completely naked as they are accustomed to be, and very modest; the other was younger, and two stout sons and five brothers and other dependents; and all the rest must have been his vassals. In his canoe he carried a man as herald. This fellow stood alone at the canoe's prow wearing a cloak of red feathers shaped like a coat of arms, and on his head he wore a great coronet of feathers which looked very fine, and in his hands he carried a white banner without any design. Two or three men had their faces painted with colors in the same pattern, and each wore on his head a large feather helmet, and on his forehead a round disk as large as a plate, and each was painted like the other in the same design and colors, so that they were uniform as in their plumes. Each held in his hand a gadget which he tinkled. There were two other men painted in another manner, and these carried two wooden trumpets all covered with birds and other designs; the wood of which they were made was very black and fine. Each of them wore a pretty helmet of green feathers very close and well put together. Six others wore helmets of white feathers, and all these were guard over the cacique's effects.

The cacique wore around his neck some ornaments of copper which they call guani, from an island in the neighborhood, and which is very fine and looks like 8-carat gold. It was in the shape of a fleur-de-lis, and as large as a plate. He wore it around his neck on a string of big beads of marble stone which they also consider of great value, and on his head he wore a coronet of small stones, green and red, arranged in order and interspersed with some bigger white ones, which looked fine; and he also wore a large jewel pendant over his forehead, and from his ears were hung two great disks of gold by some little strings of small green beads. Although he went naked he wore a girdle of the same workmanship as his coronet, but all the rest of the body was exposed. His wife was likewise adorned and naked.

When the fleet reached Hispaniola, Columbus decided to explore the southern coast. They sailed 400 miles (645 km) to the eastern tip, where the men witnessed a full eclipse of the moon on September 14. But instead of heading straight for Isabela on the northern side, the admiral turned his three ships southeast toward Puerto Rico, intending to raid Carib villages for slaves he could carry home in place of the gold he had failed to find.

Just then he was seized with a high fever, raved deliriously, and fell into a coma. His officers took control of the fleet; they gave up the rash plan to attack the Caribs and hurried the ships on to Isabela. There he seemed to recover his health, although the troublesome arthritis persisted.

It is likely that the admiral's sickness was really a mental collapse, brought on by the sense of despair over this second voyage. He could bring back to Spain no positive proof (the sailors' oath was no evidence) that he had reached the Asian mainland, nor could he show Their Majesties the gold or other riches he had promised them.

Columbus took some comfort from the presence of his two brothers in Isabela. Bartholomew had been in France when the admiral sailed on the second voyage. Reaching Seville after the fleet left, Bartholomew had placed the two sons of Columbus, Diego and Ferdinand, as pages with the queen. When the admiral's request for more men and provisions came, she put Bartholomew in command of the three caravels which had reached Isabela in the summer of 1494.

Bartholomew found that his other brother, Diego, had done a poor job of governing in the admiral's absence. One of the soldiers, Mosén Pedro Margarit, had been let loose in the interior with a band of several hundred men, instructed to live off the countryside while exploring the island for useful products. They had been told to do the Indians no harm, lest it hamper their conversion. But the soldiers went their own cruel way, robbing the Indians of their gold ornaments, raping the women, kidnapping boys and girls to serve as slaves, and gobbling up the scarce supplies of food.

When the word of these atrocities reached Diego he sent a message to Margarit ordering him to stop at once. But the man's response was to march his band of mutineers upon Isabela, seize the three ships that Bartholomew had brought from Spain, and sail for home. With him went the Benedictine, Fra Buil, whose mission it was to Christianize the heathen. But he and the other friars under his orders had done nothing to stop Margarit's brutalities or to convert the Indians.

The mutineers, sailing from Isabela before the return of Columbus, reached Spain in November 1494. Fra Buil appeared at court to denounce Columbus and his brothers and to declare there was absolutely nothing of value to be found in Hispaniola.

You will recall that earlier, in February, Columbus had sent his second-in-command, Antonio de Torres, back to Spain to secure more supplies and reinforcements. Now, near the turn of the year, de Torres sailed in to Isabela with caravels loaded with food. But this made life on the island better only briefly. For even after Margarit's and Buil's return home, Columbus had failed to regain control over the garrison. The men continued to act so brutally that the Indians rose in revolt.

In March 1495, the Columbus brothers set out to "pacify" the Indians. (That word "pacify" recurs again and again in the history books; it is used to obscure the true meaning of what exploiters do when they put down the resistance of those they exploit.) The gentle, hospitable tribes that Columbus had praised only yesterday he now set out to terrorize. With a large force of soldiers the brothers moved up into the mountains to crush Indian resistance. The Spaniards' horses and dogs, their crossbows and arquebuses overpowered the Indians, who were forced to scatter. But refusing to give up, they carried on a guerrilla war, trapping Spaniards in ambush, raiding their camps by night, and burning down their food depots.

It took almost all the year for the Spaniards to crush the last remnants of resistance. The violence of that first colonial war in the Americas was so great that it made the enslavement of the Indians possible. As the admiral's son Ferdinand boasted in his history of the Indies, now "a Spaniard could venture alone wherever he pleased, enjoy the products of the soil and the local women free of charge, and have natives carry him on their shoulders for as far as he should so desire."

Not having any gold to send to Ferdinand and Isabela, Columbus determined to fill up his ships with another source of wealth, human labor. Their value, he thought, would help repay some of the costs of his voyage, and besides, it would counter the attempt of Margarit to have the crown write off the Indies as a worthless project. The admiral sent his men on great slave raids into the interior. They rounded up 1,500 Arawaks—men, women, children—and held them captive in pens at Isabela. Since the fleet could not hold that number, the admiral selected the 500 "best specimens" to load aboard. The rest, he told the garrison, you Christians can take as slaves for your own use. Those no one wanted—about 400—were thrown out of the pens. So terrified were they that, as one of the colonists wrote, "they rushed in all directions like lunatics, women dropping and abandoning infants in the panic, running for miles without stopping, fleeing across mountains and rivers."

While this work was going on, the admiral had three more forts built in the interior. He used them as bases to control the Indians and to force them to pay him tribute in gold. He still hoped to carry large amounts of gold home on his return voyage, and by that cargo to pay dividends to the crown and the others who had invested in his Enterprise of the Indies. He still believed that somewhere, hidden deep in Hispaniola, were rich gold fields that the Indians had concealed from him.

So he ordered all Indians from the age of fourteen up, to collect a fixed amount of gold every three months. Each person who delivered his tribute of gold was given a copper token to hang around his neck. Indians found without that token had their hands cut off and were left to bleed to death.

It was an impossible, a criminal task that Columbus set. What gold was there? Mostly dust found in the beds of the island's streams. The gold ornaments worn by the Indians that the Spaniards had immediately noticed and coveted had been made slowly out of the gathering of gold dust by many generations. By now the Spaniards had robbed the Indians of all those ornaments.

Even had they been willing workers, the Indians could never have satisfied the insane demands. Forced to the unendurable hard labor, they failed to produce enough gold to satisfy the lust for it. Many Indians fled their villages and hid in the mountains. Some killed the whites wherever and whenever they could, in revenge for the tortures they suffered. And then the Spaniards, as Las Casas reported, took against them "the vengeance which the Christians called punishment, not only the murderers, but as many as might be in that village or region were punished with execution and torture."

It was an early example of the policy of "collective guilt" by which Hitler terrorized Nazi-occupied Europe during World

Top: Spaniards chopping off the hands of Indians who failed to meet the gold dust quota. From a 1619 work entitled Spanish Cruelties. *The book's engravings were taken from Bartolomé de Las Casas. Bottom: Las Casas brought the terrible report of genocide to Europe. This engraving shows the Spaniards hanging Indians and burning their homes.*

War II. If one person committed some act the Nazis disapproved of, then everyone in the family, the neighborhood, even the village was executed for it.

The fugitives in the mountains were hunted down with hounds; if they escaped capture, they often died of disease or starvation. Thousands killed themselves by taking a poison made from cassava. Many parents killed their infants to spare them a living death under Spanish rule. In only two years, half the 250,000 Indians on the island were dead. Dead by murder, dead by mutilation, dead by overwork, dead by suicide.

It was the beginning of genocide for the native population. By 1548—according to Oviedo, a Spanish nobleman who spent thirty-four years in the earliest colonial period of the Caribbean and wrote a history of the Indies—not 500 Indians remained in Hispaniola.

It was the first page in the history of the European settlement of the Americas. A beginning marked by conquest, slavery, death, a page written in blood. It makes one wonder whether Columbus Day should not be mourned, rather than celebrated.

By the fall of 1495 Ferdinand and Isabela were feeling uneasy about the Enterprise of the Indies. The many at court who disliked Columbus or who had returned from the Indies dissatisfied with his rule, had lobbied effectively against him. The monarchs decided to send someone out to look into the facts. In October four caravels anchored off Isabela, carrying supplies and the chief investigator, Juan Aguado. Columbus stood by patiently while Aguado took testimony from the colonists, most of them sick, unhappy, and eager to go home.

The colony had been established more than eighteen months ago on this large and fertile island. Yet it had failed to become self-sustaining and was always demanding more men and supplies. Its energies, Aguado found, had gone into looting, searching for gold, and catching slaves.

What had gone wrong? First, though Columbus meant to build a permanent settlement, that was not the intention of his colonists. They came to trade trinkets for gold and to plunder the island and return home with the loot. When they did not grow rich overnight, they were bitterly let down and wanted out.

Then, too, the upper class of Spanish colonists—the "gentlemen," or hidalgos—were not used to manual labor. They had only contempt for those who worked with their hands. They would rather rot than do anything for themselves. They were helpless without artisans and farmers to make do for them. In a land where it was easy to grow food, easy to catch fish or fowl, they acted as though Hispaniola were some godforsaken desert.

And finally, their tradition as warriors, always engaged in fighting, made them ripe for the arrogance that marked the conquistadors. It explains to a degree their brutality, their cold indifference to the suffering of the Indians, their harshness even toward one another.

Columbus decided he must go back to Spain to defend himself against all charges. In March 1496 he sailed from Isabela on the *Niña,* accompanied by the newly built ship the *Santa Cruz.* The two caravels were terribly overcrowded with 225 Spaniards and thirty Indians. The admiral chose a poor route home this time, and it was June—three months—before the passengers, near starvation, sailed into Cádiz.

14

Columbus in Chains

What did that second voyage achieve?

Very little, in Columbus's own mind. When he came ashore at Cadiz he put on not the gorgeous costume appropriate to a great admiral, but the coarse brown dress of a Franciscan friar. It seemed to be his way of signifying that humility had replaced arrogance. But viewed from the perspective of empire builders, Columbus had added still other island colonies to Spain's possessions, and had found Jamaica, which would later become a most prized possession not of the Spanish but of the British Empire. Besides, he had planted the first European settlement on this side of the Atlantic. More personally, the historians rank highly the skill the admiral displayed at navigating in both coastal and deep waters.

For Columbus this was not enough. After two voyages he had still failed to meet with the grand rulers of Asia or to see that continent's legendary splendors. The oath he had forced his men to take to certify *his* version of geography only made him appear ridiculous.

The discovery of new islands of the Indies created no sensation at court. The fact that he could repeat his first voyage somehow diminished the original achievement. Yes, scholars were interested in reports of the second voyage, but most others were indifferent. What did a few sick Indian slaves amount to as the payoff for so large an investment? Some even began to wonder if these islands of the Indies were really part of Asia. Perhaps the Portuguese were right about that, after all. The new islands in the West were surely much further from mainland Asia than Columbus believed. When Peter Martyr read the reports of the first voyage he wrote in 1494 that "when treating of this country one must speak of a new world, so distant is it and so devoid of civilization and religion."

Other European powers, particularly in Portugal and England, began to send explorers to regions outside the Caribbean, into the North Atlantic. Old stories circulated of islands west of Ireland. For years now ships had left the English port of Bristol to fish on the Grand Banks in the western Atlantic. Perhaps they had reached the mainland of North America? In 1496, after the news of Columbus's first voyage, Henry VII had licensed John Cabot, an Italian mariner, to explore the western North Atlantic. He followed a course somewhat south of the Viking route across the ocean, but we know nothing of what he found. In his next voyage he did report land, possibly Newfoundland. And in a final expedition, in 1498, he sailed past Newfoundland and Nova Scotia, reaching New England. (His findings are shown on de la Cosa's map of 1500.) Cabot's projects brought no commercial returns, so the English investors lost interest for a time.

In 1495, the Portuguese decided to send a fleet to India, but not until 1497 did it actually sail. Vasco da Gama headed the fleet of four ships, under instructions to trade and not only to explore. His was a superb feat of seamanship. Learning from Dias's experience, he sailed far out into the Atlantic until he passed the trade wind belts, before turning east and steering for the Cape of Good Hope. He rounded the Cape and then stopped at East African ports, where he picked up water and fuel and a Moslem pilot who was a master of celestial navigation. With his help he crossed the Indian Ocean to Calicut, where he loaded on a cargo of pepper and cinnamon. Then he sailed for home. His voyage lasted two years, with about 300 days of it spent at sea. He was out of sight of land for ninety-six days and traveled about 4,500 miles (7,240 km) between landfalls. It was a much longer journey than the 2,600 miles (4,185 km) Columbus sailed in thirty-six days beyond sight of land.

When da Gama came home in 1499 to report his success, the Portuguese government made detailed plans to organize commerce with Asia, and to dispatch annual fleets under royal charter. The costs of that trade proved very high, but the profits were enormous.

Columbus had no such achievement to report. Not even the settlement at Isabela could be called a success. The admiral lacked the experience and the temperament to be an effective colonial governor. While he was absent in Spain, his brother Bartholomew abandoned Isabela and persuaded some of the Spaniards to begin building a new settlement on the island's south coast. This became the city of Santo Domingo; for fifty years it would be the capital of the Spanish Indies.

Columbus stayed quietly in Cadiz, living in the house of Bernaldez, the curate and historian. There he rested and rebuilt his health while recounting his adventures to the priest and arranging to leave his journals with him. In July the monarchs sent word they would receive the admiral at court, now in Burgos. He set forth with the Indian slaves in tow, adorning them for the journey with the gold ornaments he had taken away. It was a show to convince the Spaniards that there was indeed plenty of gold in Hispaniola.

The king and queen welcomed him graciously if not enthusiastically. They listened to his story and then read the sealed document Aguado had sent, a report loud with complaints. Ignoring his enemies at court, Columbus promptly proposed a third voyage. He asked for eight ships this time, two to return at once to Hispaniola with supplies, and six for himself to lead later on. What helped his case were reports that the king of Portugal believed a mainland existed in the Atlantic south or southwest of Columbus's islands, directly across the ocean from Africa. It was a story that the Admiral himself had heard from Indians. If this huge landmass did exist, would it come under the dominion of Spain or Portugal, according to the Treaty of Tordesillas? The court cosmographer, Ferrer de Blanes, wanted the matter looked into. He advised the crown that this was a most important matter for Columbus to investigate on his third voyage.

Their Majesties were in no hurry, however. It would be two years before the third expedition was ready to leave. No one was excited by the venture. What Columbus had promised in newfound wealth had never materialized. Spaniards were no longer eager to share in the glory of discovery, and the lure of profit was long gone. The sovereigns had their own costly troubles, fighting wars and arranging dynastic marriages.

Finally, plans for the expedition were completed. Columbus was to take 300 men at royal expense to Hispaniola, and fifty more if he could get them to pay their own way. The men included hidalgos, artisans, miners, soldiers, laborers, farmers, gardeners—all at specified rates of pay. There were to be thirty women too (one for each ten men), but only if they agreed to work for their passage. Whether any sailed with the fleet we do not know.

Because no one could be sure how many men would volunteer for the expedition, the crown offered free pardons to jailed criminals who would agree to stay at least one year in the islands. (Again, we do not know how many accepted the offer. Recruiting convicts became, however, a basic practice in Spanish colonial settlement.)

The fleet sailed in late May 1498. (At that very moment, Vasco da Gama arrived in Calicut on the coast of India.) Three of the ships headed directly for Hispaniola with fresh provisions. The other three, commanded by Columbus, took a route south of the equator, to check on the rumors of that unidentified mainland. The admiral descended to the latitude of Guinea, then sailed out to the Cape Verde Islands. The fleet was becalmed in those waters and suffered such steaming heat that it broke open the wine and water casks and spoiled their food. The crews were so exhausted by this strange ordeal that the admiral decided to shift his course north, to more familiar waters. Had he continued his original plan, he would have found the Amazon River basin and the continent of South America—the mainland the Portuguese suspected lay across from Africa.

The fleet was now sailing somewhat parallel to the South American coast, though at a considerable distance, heading northeast. On July 31 Columbus sighted a big island he named Trinidad. The crews were relieved to see land at last, but as the fleet neared the coast a host of Indians came out in canoes and shot arrows at the strangers. Better to stay aboard ship: the fleet went around the island and entered the Gulf of Paria. It is that gulf, on the coast of Venezuela, into which the Orinoco River spills. From his flagship the admiral could see promontories and bays that were part of the South American continent. But so conditioned was he to wandering among islands that he failed to recognize this as the continent the Portuguese had speculated was there.

While the admiral stayed aboard ship he sent some men ashore in search of badly needed fresh water. They found a strange new plant—corn—and met Indians whose arms were ornamented with large pearls. Nearby were islands such as Margarita (the word in Spanish for "pearl") where big beds of pearl oysters grew. Although Columbus was the first European to find them, he ignored these natural riches. Only later did Spain profit from harvesting them.

Coming out of the gulf, the fleet sailed through the narrow passage between the mainland and Trinidad and headed west, following the coastline of South America. When they reached Margarita, Columbus set the course northwest across the Caribbean for Hispaniola.

While sailing on the Gulf of Paria, Columbus was struck by the great quantity of its fresh water. A ship had to sail 20 miles (32 km) off the coast before it reached salt water. He realized

that a river (it was the Orinoco) which could push its water that far out to sea must be big and powerful. Could an island be vast enough to contain so great a river? Or was the Orinoco flowing out of a continent? He came that close to recognizing that he had found a continent in the west that no European knew about.

Instead of grappling with the facts, Columbus's mind spun off in fantasy. In a dispatch he would later send from Hispaniola, he wrote: "The Scriptures tell us that in the Earthly Paradise grows the tree of life, and that from it flows the source that gives rise to the four great rivers, the Ganges, the Tigris, the Euphrates, and the Nile. The Earthly Paradise, which no one can reach except by the will of God, lies at the end of the Orient. And that is where we are." Steeped in the medieval tradition, he believed he was close by the Garden of Eden, the site of the Creation. This gulf, whose fresh waters he had just crossed, must be the mouth of the Ganges. What was actually the coast of Venezuela he took to be, like Cuba, part of the Asian continent. The observed facts could not break into his dream of the Orient. Good luck had brought him to the edge of the New World, but he was unable to believe it.

He went on to cite all the ancient authors whose pages he had long devoured, in order to bolster his argument. God, he hoped, would "forgive those who libel this noble Enterprise and who oppose it." How little had his work cost the crown, he continued, and yet now Their Majesties have "another world" in which to spread the Holy Faith. "I tell all the people here of the nobility of all Christians," wrote this devout soul.

Indians harvesting pearl oysters off the Caribbean islands, with Spanish ships taking them aboard for sale in Europe

The fleet arrived at Hispaniola in mid-August 1498, three months after leaving Spain. Bartholomew showed his brother the new colony of Santo Domingo (named after their father), where a few hundred settlers lived. But the news was bad. The Indians were dying off, destroyed by slave raids and forced labor and hunger. The Spaniards were still fighting among themselves. A majority of them had risen in revolt against the Columbus brothers (there were now three of them, for the youngest, Diego, had also settled in Hispaniola). The leader of the rebels, Francisco Roldan, had found allies among the Indians when he promised them no more slave raids and no gold tribute.

Roldan liked the Indians' gentle way of life and enjoyed the natural beauty and the freedom of this island realm. Unlike Columbus, he did not hunger for power and wealth. The admiral tried to crush the revolt but had fewer men to support him than Roldan had. So he gave in to the rebels and offered amnesty for past actions and ships for them to return to Spain. Anyone who preferred to stay would be given free land. Roldan agreed to the terms; Columbus had lost. An inept administrator, Columbus had acted like a tyrant, trying to impose his will by violence. Those "foreigners"—as the settlers called the Columbus brothers—"were always quick to torture, hang, and behead."

For two years Columbus struggled to stay in power, while appealing often to Their Majesties for more ships, more supplies, more men. The sovereigns began to feel the admiral was going mad. His letters were neither lucid nor confident. He had lost control of the colony and of himself. Ferdinand refused to send more help to a doomed enterprise. And Isabella, growing old and sick, and in despair over the sudden deaths of two of her three children she had happily married off only recently, could no longer care what happened to Columbus.

The court decided to send over a commissioner, Francisco de Bobadilla, to take charge of Hispaniola. When he arrived at Santo Domingo in August 1500, the first thing he saw was the corpses of two Spaniards swinging from the gallows—executed for rebellion, with five more to follow. Another uprising had begun, led by a follower of Roldan, and Columbus and Bartholomew were in the interior, hunting down rebels. Bobadilla reprieved the captured rebels at once, and locking up Diego, who refused to obey his orders, began an investigation.

The admiral returned to find everything changed. Angered by this threat to his dominion, he challenged Bobadilla's credentials and demanded the commissioner take orders from *him*. Bobadilla replied by ordering Columbus to be taken prisoner. The haughty admiral asked who would dare touch him. Then I'll put you in chains, Bobadilla said. No one had the spirit to do it, until the admiral's cook, stone-faced, stepped forward to put irons around Columbus's wrists and ankles.

Placing the three brothers under guard in the citadel, Bobadilla took control of the colony and conducted a rapid inquiry into its affairs. He decided that the brothers must be given a full trial in Spain. They were shipped out of Santo Domingo early in October 1500. Once at sea, the ship's captain offered to remove the chains, but Columbus refused. Their majesties had ordered him placed in chains, and he would wear them until royal command removed them.

The ship made swift passage and docked at Cádiz late in October. The admiral disembarked in chains, as though they were his proudest possession. He was taken to Seville, still in chains, to enter a Carthusian monastery. Word soon reached the king and queen in Cordova of the admiral's arrival, and they at once ordered Columbus to be set free. They were angry with Bobadilla for going to such an extreme in executing his authority. They sent 2,000 ducats to Columbus "so that he could appear in court in a state befitting a person of his rank." Pleased at this treatment, he expected a prompt hearing. But he waited for months before they summoned him to court in Granada.

When he walked into the Alhambra and stood before Ferdinand and Isabella, he said nothing for a long time. Then he fell on his knees before them and wept. They told him to rise and speak his mind. Whatever mistakes he had made, were made without evil intent. Had he not been loyal all these years? Had he not done his best? But then he exploded into a tirade against Bobadilla and loudly protested all the grievances he had been made to suffer. He demanded that Bobadilla be punished and that he, Columbus, be reinstated as governor, with all his rights and property restored.

Although to others in the court it was plain that Columbus had not made a winning case for himself, the admiral felt pleased with his performance. He was sure that everything he asked would be granted. It was another sign of his loosening hold on reality. How could he be wrong about anything when God had chosen him to carry out his sacred mission? His course was guided by a heavenly hand. It would never lead him into harm.

As he waited in the gardens of Granada for a reply from the king and queen, they were busy with far more urgent matters. The Enterprise of the Indies no longer seemed important. Nor was discovery now the sole province of Columbus. He had shown the way, yes, but many others were following his course. Almost yearly other explorers were crossing the seas. Some went further south than he had, to the more distant shores of South America. Peralonso Niño had discovered the Amazon River. Rodrigo de Batidas had entered the Gulf of Darien, at Panama. Cabral on the way to India had touched the coast of southern Brazil. And far to the north, Cabot had reached New England. Ojeda, one of the admiral's former lieutenants, entered the Gulf of Paria and began the commercialization of the pearl oyster beds. With him on that voyage went the Florentine Amerigo Vespucci, who would write superb accounts of this and other voyages. Ten years later, with Columbus dead, the new maps would name the lands of the western hemisphere "America." Thus the reporter, and not the explorer, was honored.

As the news of these voyages spread, a geographer, Duarte Pacheco Pereira, suggested that "a continuous landmass" ran from Labrador in the north down to the Rio de la Plata in the

Some of the great voyagers of Columbus's time.
From left: Diaz del Castillo Bernal, Vasco
da Gama, Amerigo Vespucci, Ferdinand Magellan.

south. Columbus noted the outcome of each voyage and plotted it on a map. To any objective observer these findings pointed to the existence of an unforeseen continent. But Columbus could not accept that. Surely he had reached the edge of Asia, not some unknown continent. How could he and all the old authors he had relied on be wrong?

It came to him that none of the recent explorers had gone west of the islands he had found. South, yes, and one or two north. But not *west*. Since he had convinced himself that Cuba was a peninsula of China on the Asian continent, he figured there must be a large body of water between Cuba and the Gulf of Darien, a passage that had not yet been explored. This, he thought, would be the strait through which Marco Polo had sailed from China into the Indian Ocean.

For two years he argued for just one more chance, to find that passage and the Indies. But who would be eager to give him another fleet? So many other explorers had shown they could do as well or better than the admiral and find new lands. Both Cabral and de Gama had commanded Portuguese expeditions to India and established a steady sea route to those markets. The monopoly of the Italian merchant cities was broken.

Instead of saying yes to Columbus, Ferdinand and Isabella told him he was through as governor of the Indies. They replaced him with Nicolás de Ovando, though without giving him the titles of admiral or viceroy. Columbus retained those titles but it was understood they were only honors now and carried no authority. The crown made Ovando governor of Hispaniola, replacing Bobadilla, and sent him out with a fleet of thirty-two ships and 2,500 men, commanded by Antonio de Torres.

When Ovando arrived, he was greeted by a woman *cacique,* Anacoana, heading a delegation of eighty-four other chiefs. The Spaniards turned the welcoming party into a massacre. They attacked the Indians offering peace, killed everyone they could catch, burned down the house of Anacoana, and hanged her. Within a few years Hispaniola was made into a stronghold from which the Spaniards would send out forces to commit the same horrors upon the Indian people of Cuba.

While removing his authority, the king and queen ensured that Columbus would continue to receive his agreed-upon share of income from the territories of the Indies. At fifty, feeling old, and with illness steadily weakening him, he could have retired to a very comfortable life in a castle of Spain. He held high titles, his income made him rich, his reputation was international. Why struggle for more? But he could never relent in his pursuit of the goal Providence had set for him. He believed there were great new discoveries to be made and *he* was the man to make them.

He worked out a plan for a fourth voyage. It was lost at court. He drafted another, and this time the sovereigns gave in. Perhaps they were weary of his constant buzzing in their ears and wanted to get him out of Spain. The crown would provide the ships, and Genoese backers seem to have offered some money. Their message to Columbus said that he was not to exercise any authority they had removed. He was to search for gold and silver, pearls and spices, but was ordered not to send back any Indians as slaves. Nor could he stop at Hispaniola, unless it should prove necessary and only on his return voyage.

Nothing was said about his chief reason for the voyage—to find the passage to the Indies.

15

The Last Voyage

To find the passage to the Indies? But had he not already found it? Were not all these islands outlying parts of the Indies? And Cuba even a part of the mainland? Was Columbus admitting, silently, that he had not yet reached Asia? On each of the three previous voyages he had reported success, yet without convincing proof. Adequate for himself, maybe, but not for others. Always there had been doubts and even denials.

On May 9, 1502, he sailed from Cádiz with a small fleet of four caravels. The crews numbered 140; a fourth of them would never come home. A majority of the crew were boys, some only twelve or thirteen. Columbus himself was too old and ill to command the fleet. That task was assigned to Diego Triana, an old friend. Columbus took along his younger son, Ferdinand, twelve years old, and his brother Bartholomew. We know much about this voyage, chiefly from Ferdinand's account, written long after, and from a somewhat hysterical letter written by Columbus.

In the swiftest of all his voyages—twenty days—he made landfall at the island of Martinique. There he stayed a few days, taking on water supplies. Then, unable to resist visiting Hispaniola, despite royal orders not to, he headed for the island and landed close by, but not at, the port of Santo Domingo. He sent a message to Ovando asking permission to enter the port in order to trade an adequate ship for a better one. And he warned Ovando that a hurricane was about to strike that part of Hispaniola and would sink Columbus's ships if they didn't find shelter in the port.

Ovando had been told to keep Columbus away, so he refused permission to come into port while ignoring the hurricane warning. Columbus knew from unhappy experience how devastating such a storm could be and immediately brought his own ships into shelter some leagues from Santo Domingo. At the same time twenty ships of the fleet that Ovando had arrived with two months before had just sailed out to the open sea for the trip back to Spain. They were utterly destroyed by the hurricane. All the ships went down in minutes; over 500 lives were lost. (Among the drowned were Bobadilla and Roldan, old enemies of Columbus. When the admiral heard of their death, he took it as divine punishment for their opposition to him.)

After riding out the storm, and repairing the minor damage to his ships, Columbus headed west in the Caribbean, hoping to find the Asian continent by sailing past what he thought was the peninsula of Cuba. He reached the bay island of Bonacca (now Guanaja) off the coast of Honduras. When Bartholomew took a few men ashore, they saw how much more advanced these island natives were. They were expert weavers and metalworkers and used copper tools and utensils. They dressed in dyed woven tunics and cotton robes. The women wore shawls and as weapons the men used powerful battle-axes and long flint-edged swords. The Spaniards watched the natives using quantities of small, unfamiliar beans as currency. (This was Europe's first glimpse of the cacao bean.) The Indians traveled on the sea in very large and well-made dugout canoes, fitted with an enclosed cabin. The boats must have been used for coastal trading.

Of course Columbus could not know that Bonacca was a small outpost of the great Mayan empire. Had he headed north he would soon have come upon the Yucatan and the heart of the Mayan civilization. But he seized some of the merchandise, held one Indian as a guide, and turned southeast instead, coasting along Honduras as he searched for the passage to the Indies he had calculated must be there. This leg of the voyage was hard going: drenching rains, high winds, great storms. For four weeks they were battered, their sails ripped, their anchors lost, their shrouds and hawsers torn.

The desperate seamen prayed constantly and vowed to make pilgrimages if the Lord would see them safely through this hell. Young Ferdinand suffered terribly, and the admiral himself came close to death. In those twenty-eight days the ships made only 170 miles (275 km). The sailors were frantic to turn back, to get the awful winds behind them, but Columbus would not give up now. How could he miss this last chance to find the passage to the Asian mainland? So the four caravels inched along the coasts of what are now Nicaragua and Costa Rica. When the winds eased up for a bit, sailors went ashore, where they saw pumas, deer, monkeys, and crocodiles at the river mouths. They met Indians somewhat different-looking from the Arawaks. They painted their faces red and black and bored large holes in their ears.

On October 5 the fleet came to a channel which Columbus was sure must be the passage he yearned to find. But it was only a large lagoon rimmed by mountains. Now called the Chiriqui Lagoon, it is an inland salt lake not far from where the Panama Canal would be cut some 400 years later. Just across the mountains lay the Pacific Ocean. Had Columbus crossed the isthmus of Panama, there would still have been about half the circumference of the earth between him and Asia.

As they were sailing along the coast of Central America, the crews going ashore found gold in the form of large disks the Indians wore round their necks. In the villages the Spaniards traded their trinkets for the gold ornaments. Columbus later wrote the king and queen that he had learned of vast gold mines, vast beyond belief, in a valley called Veragua (now Panama). His

Mayan sculpture from Palenque, Mexico.
Columbus just missed finding that civilization.

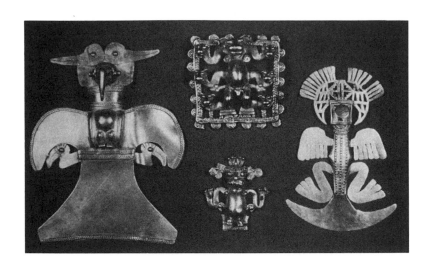

*From the great Indian cultures of the pre-Columbian
era came such gold ornaments as these. The center pieces
are from Panama, the right and left from Colombia.*

letter becomes lyrical. "Gold is the most excellent, gold is treasure, and who has it can do whatever he likes in this world.
With it he can bring souls to Paradise. . . ."

Now, he thought, he was at Ptolemy's Golden Peninsula,
and nearby must be the Cochin China of Marco Polo. But instead of going on until he found it, he stopped to find the gold.
There really was gold about 20 miles (32 km) away, in the
mountains. The Indians, not having mining tools, could only
scratch bits of it from the earth with their knives. The gold lay
in high mountains covered with dense tropical forest. The climate was intolerable. To extract the gold would require so huge
an investment that no one could do it profitably.

The difficulties did not stop Columbus. He began building
a colony at Belén, on the coast, to serve as a base from which
to exploit the gold fields. His men had to fight jungle, rains,
floods, heat, and the Indians who were soon turned from friend
to enemy by "a thousand outrages," as Ferdinand put it.

After three months at Veragua, Columbus decided to leave Bartholomew in command of the base while he himself went on to Hispaniola with three of the ships. Trouble with the Indians broke out in open warfare, and Columbus through ambush captured some thirty Indians to take with him. He confined them below deck on one of the ships. But even as he prepared to sail, the Indians chose suicide rather than captivity. During the night they all hanged themselves from beams in the low hold of the ship, bending their knees while they strangled. Much later, writing of it, the admiral's son Ferdinand disposed of the tragedy by saying, "Their deaths were not great harm to the ships. . . ."

On shore, the Indians attacked Bartholomew and the men Columbus was leaving behind to build the new colony and extract the gold. They wounded Bartholomew and killed many others. The survivors managed to get out to the fleet on a hastily built raft. On April 16, 1503, Columbus left Veragua, never to return. Delirious with malaria, he gave up all hope of accomplishing anything more on this final voyage. The fleet headed back to Santo Domingo to have the ships repaired and to take on provisions for the journey back to Spain.

They had been away a year. Their three ships were now leaky tubs, rotting from colonies of mollusks that had penetrated the hulls during the long stay at Veragua. The crews pumped day and night to keep the ships afloat. They had to abandon one as it was about to sink. The other two were battered by a storm while they were still 200 miles (320 km) from Santo Domingo. Columbus ordered the pilots to head for Jamaica at once. Late in June they beached the two hulks at Saint Ann's Bay on the north coast of the island.

What could Columbus expect now? With 116 exhausted Spaniards he was stranded on an empty beach, ships ruined, supplies gone.

Here he would stay for one long year. A year that would do nothing to advance his goal, a year that would only diminish his reputation.

Columbus knew from his second voyage that Jamaica was peopled by Indians of the same cultures as those of Cuba and the Bahamas. He knew too that there was no gold on this island. Fearing that his men would get into trouble with the Indians, he ordered them to stay close to the cabins they had built out of the ships' hulks. They would all have starved to death if the Indians had not brought them food. It seems strange to us that the Spaniards did nothing to feed themselves by fishing or by hunting game.

How would they get home? They had neither the skills nor the tools to fell timber and build a ship out of it. Or to replace the rotten planks of the old ships. Nor was such hard labor to the taste of most of them. Far off in Hispaniola, the Spaniards had no idea where Columbus was, and there was no reason to expect a searching party would ever find them. The likelihood of other explorers coming across them by chance was very small. The only way they could be rescued was for someone to reach Hispaniola by Indian canoe and there obtain a caravel to carry them all back to Spain.

Columbus knew it was urgent to reach Hispaniola quickly. The Indians might tire of providing food, and the Spaniards would surely turn quarrelsome. It would be a risky journey for anyone to take: over 400 miles (640 km) of paddling from here to Santo Domingo. No one wanted to attempt it. Finally Diego Méndez and Bartolomo Fieschi took two dugout canoes and, with six other Spaniards, and ten Indians each to do the paddling, started out in the hope that at least one of them would make it. Fieschi's crew quit when they touched Hispaniola, with 350 more miles (560 km) to paddle along the shore before reaching Santo Domingo. But Méndez made it, bringing the news to Ovando that Columbus was marooned on Jamaica.

For seven months Ovando did nothing about Columbus; he was too occupied with butchering the Indians. He refused to let Méndez take the one small ship in port. Instead, he made him wait many months for ships to come in from Spain.

Over eight months passed on Jamaica without word from Méndez. One day a caravel arrived, but only to stay one day to see what Columbus was up to. It left some wine and pork, and the news that Méndez was safe and would send a rescue party when he could obtain a ship. Meanwhile, as the men continued to wait, hope faded and a mutiny boiled up. Two men, the Porras brothers, led the conspiracy. Defying Columbus, and almost murdering him, they broke free and paddled off toward Hispaniola in ten Indian canoes. They stopped at villages along the Jamaican coast, robbing the Indians of supplies. They began crossing to Hispaniola when a storm so terrified them that they threw their supplies overboard, and then the Indian paddlers too. The Indians, who clung desperately to the gunwales, had their hands hacked off by the Spaniards. Only a few men were spared to steer the canoes. They landed at the nearest beach, where they stayed a month, harassing the Indians. Then, giving up all hope of reaching Hispaniola, they trudged back to Columbus on foot.

The admiral tried to make peace with the mutineers, but they made such demands it was impossible. Bartholomew, with fifty armed men, took them on and won the brief battle. Many were killed or wounded; the rest, surrendering, were granted full pardon.

It was June 1504 before Méndez was able to charter a small and leaky ship that had arrived at Santo Domingo from Spain. It sailed to Jamaica to pick up the marooned men and take them back to Santo Domingo. There a better ship was chartered. On September 12, Columbus, with his son and brother and twenty-two others sailed for Spain. The rest of the survivors decided to remain, at least for a while.

It was a long journey home. Fifty-six days at sea passed before the admiral's ship docked in the Spanish harbor. The date was November 7, 1504. Ferdinand, thirteen when this voyage began, was now sixteen. And the admiral was fifty-three.

16

Changing the World

Coming ashore in Spain, Columbus was a worn old man. Wracked by fever, gout, arthritis, he could barely walk. He was brought to Seville, and moved into a rented house. Servants took care of him, for he was well off and could easily afford it. To his son Diego, now a member of the king's guard, he wrote complaining that income was still owed him from the commerce of the Indies. Diego, an experienced courtier, was unable to get him the audience with Ferdinand and Isabella that his father demanded. One reason was the queen's terminal illness. She died about a month after Columbus returned to Spain.

Now he had lost his best friend at court. But ever hopeful, he expected that in her will she would restore all his privileges and authority. In May of 1505 he was carried by mule the 300 miles (480 km) from Seville to Segovia, where the court was staying. This time the king agreed to hear him out, and Columbus presented his appeal for the income and property he believed due him. The archbishop of Seville was asked by the king to settle the affair. In the end, Columbus's share of returns on commerce was interpreted so as to considerably reduce his income. His request for restoration to power as viceroy and governor of the Indies was refused in the interests of the state, which thought he had been a disaster in those roles.

So he lost his last battle and returned to his sickbed, worse than before. Nevertheless, he was a rich man. The crown's treasurers did not cheat him; he continued to receive the revenue due him. His estate became quite valuable. He did not spend his last years in poverty, as the legend has it.

He moved from Segovia to Valladolid, 60 miles (almost 100 km) away, where the climate would be better for him, and where the friars of the nearby monastery of St. Francis could take care of him. He spent his last days, unhappy ones, in a small brick house and died on May 20, 1505. With him were his brothers and his sons. No one from court was present, although the king was staying at a castle only a few miles off. In the daily civic register of Valladolid there is no mention of the admiral's death.

His funeral procession was small; it might have been any gentleman of no importance going to his grave. No distinguished people attended, and no notice was given of his passing. It is not known where his remains lie now. They could be in Seville, in Santo Domingo, in Havana—or in none of these places. This part of his history is a mystery too. His contemporaries seemed quickly to forget him. Not until the mid-nineteenth century would his fame be revived. Until that time no marker, no monument, no stone was placed anywhere in the Americas to recognize his deeds. In 1845, Pius IX, the first pope to cross the Atlantic, noted the long silence about Columbus as "history's terrible contradiction."

Why this indifference? Look at it from the perspective of the year 1500. The very fact of America's existence was a radically new thing. It was far beyond the range of European experience. No one expected such a discovery. About Africa and Asia they knew a little something. But about America? About those strange beings, the Indians? Their existence challenged all the preconceptions of Europeans. Little wonder if it took a long time to bring America into focus.

We saw early on that the news of Columbus's landfall in the Indies caused some excitement. His first letter was printed many times by the year 1500. And the reports of later explorers appeared soon after, rousing much curiosity. One man, Juan Luis Vives, born in the year of America's discovery, wrote in 1531 that "truly, the globe has been opened up to the human race."

Still, little attention was paid to Columbus himself. Almost no one probed into his personality or investigated his career. The event of his death, as we've seen, was not even recorded in the city where he had lived. What helped keep his name alive was the biography his son Fernando published in 1571. Some wondered why no statue was erected to Columbus when so many others had received that tribute. What such admirers centered on was not the voyage itself but the gold this sailor had sent to Spain, and the prospect he opened up of mass conversion to the Catholic faith in the New World.

Only slowly was Columbus transformed into a legendary hero. Some epic poems appearing in Italy in the late 1500s chose him as the central figure, and in 1614 the great Spanish dramatist Lope de Vega made him the hero of a play. He treated Columbus as a visionary dreamer, ridiculed by the world, who becomes the symbol of the spirit of discovery.

The conversion of Columbus into a romantic hero often was coupled with portraits of the man as a divinely appointed instrument to spread God's word to the far corners of the globe. Scholars who have studied the early treatment of Columbus in world literature find relatively little interest shown in him. Many memoirs and chronicles make no mention of the New World for a century after Columbus. As the historian J. H. Elliott puts it, "It is as if, at a certain point, the mental shutters come down; as if, with so much to see and absorb and understand, the effort suddenly becomes too much for them, and Europeans retreat to the half-light of their traditional mental world."

Elliott points out that this sixteenth-century response has many historical parallels. "The attempt by any society to comprehend another inevitably forces it to reappraise itself," he says. And that process is often painful, for it requires giving up many traditional notions and inherited ideas. The emergence of the Renaissance from the Middle Ages was just such a time. Scholars worshipped antiquity to the point of slavishness. They invoked authority to shut out or discount new experience. Our minds, our imaginations—today as well as then, though perhaps to a lesser degree—are preconditioned. We tend to see what we are expected to see, and to ignore or reject whatever we are mentally unprepared for.

There may have been other voyages in the early 1500s to the same general region Columbus reached, voyages we have no record of. It seems likely, for maps of that time show many fairly accurate coastal features which can't be linked to any voyage whose records have come down to us. But year by year, exploration and maybe some guessing added details that gave greater solidity and reality to the New World. At the same time, Columbus's belief in a seaway to the more developed parts of Asia became less and less plausible. The New World, cartographers were soon suggesting, was not a string of islands but a continental landmass. It had no connection to Asia. Rather, it was a continent, a great region of the globe, existing on its own, separate from Europe, Africa, and Asia.

What those first tentative maps showed was soon combined into the great world map produced in woodcut by the geographer Martin Waldseemüller at Lorraine in 1507. Only a single copy of this map survives, although perhaps a thousand copies of the original were published. It shows the New World in two parts—northern and southern continents, with the southern much the bigger. A narrow strait separates the two on the main map, but on an inset map a continuous isthmus connects them. To the east of the New World lies the Atlantic Ocean, and to the west, another great sea (the Pacific).

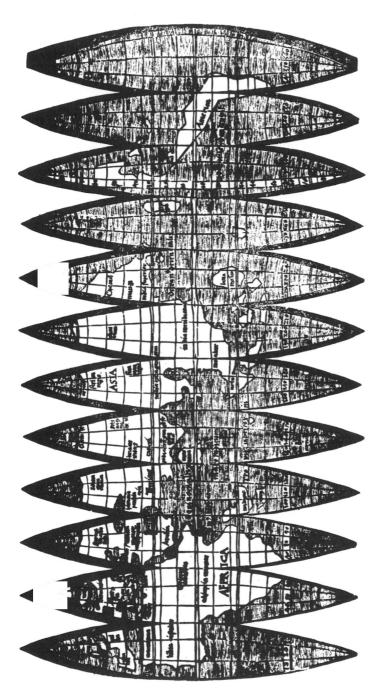

Drawn in 1507 by the geographer Martin Waldseemüller, this segmented map was designed to fit together into a sphere. In the white space at far right is the name America, used for the first time to designate the land Columbus found.

The map makers began the general practice of using "America" for the newly discovered lands when he gave the New World that name. It was the enduring effect of *Mundus Novus,* a pamphlet which gave a vivid account of Amerigo Vespucci's two voyages to America in the wake of Columbus. Published in 1502–1504, it went through many editions and appeared in five languages, reaching many more readers than Columbus's letter. It fixed in many readers' minds the true belief that a new continent had been found—a barrier between Europe and Asia—and the mistaken belief that Amerigo Vespucci had discovered it. The name America was at first attached to the southern continent. Later in the century the geographer Gerardus Mercator's maps and globes extended the name to North America as well.

While what Columbus did radically changed the way the world looked at itself, it took centuries for the actual documents to become widely known. Historians of the admiral's own day—Las Casas and Bernaldez—wrote much about him, and their work has been cited here. But the book by Las Casas, though written in 1550, was not published until 1870. And the manuscript by Bernaldez, to whom Columbus confided his experience, was not published until 1875. The ship's log that the admiral kept, as it was abstracted by Las Casas, was not printed until 1825.

The reputation of Columbus has had its ups and downs over the centuries. In 1554 Lopez de Gómara claimed Columbus had achieved "the greatest thing since the creation of the world." Much later, in 1768, a Massachusetts writer, Cornelius de Pauw, said that "the discovery of the New World has been the most disastrous event in the history of mankind." Applying a moral judgment, he blamed Columbus and the Spanish for the spread of slavery in the New World. Could it be called progress when millions of people were forced into such miserable, painful, and hopeless existence?

It took over 300 years before the first American biography of Columbus appeared. When Washington Irving published his

Life and Voyages of Columbus in 1828 it became an internationally popular book. Scholars dug into the scattered archives for more evidence, and before the century was out the log, the letters, the reports, and other documents about the man and his voyages were being gathered, studied, and published.

Those who interpreted history as the outcome of the will of Providence, saw Columbus as the instrument of God to spread the gospel throughout the New World. The Catholic Church considered him for beatification in the late nineteenth century, but the church tribunal decided against it. Only one ballot was cast in favor. His introduction of slavery into America, his concubinage with Beatrice de Harana, and the cheating of the sailor Triana out of a lifetime pension for being the first to sight land all weighed against Columbus. But for better or worse, almost everyone now accepted that the bold Genoese had been the first European to discover the New World.

The backing Ferdinand and Isabella gave Columbus was inspired by the hope of great wealth to be gained from establishing trading centers in the Indies. By the death of Columbus the dream of riches had begun to fade. The great change came when in 1519 Hernán Cortés led a small expedition from Cuba to Mexico, where he shattered an Aztec kingdom of fabulous wealth and a level of civilization far more complex than Columbus had encountered in the Caribbean. Within a few years the first large shipment of treasure reached Spain to open a new age for the Empire.

A decade later Francisco Pizarro conquered the Inca empire of Peru and opened its great riches to Spanish exploitation. Quickly Spanish control radiated from the original Caribbean bases founded by Columbus throughout South America and then up into the southern and southwestern regions of North America. Within a generation the geographical misconceptions of Columbus were finally corrected.

But how much did it profit Spain? Treasure in the form of gold had been what the crown sought. Only Colombia, however, was a major gold producer. It was silver mines of Peru and Mexico that became the mainstay of Spanish wealth. Silver ore was extracted with mercury, a process that devastated the slaves. By mercury poisoning and silicosis, first the Indians and later the Africans forced to labor died off. Although Spain made travel and trade with the colonies into a royal monopoly, the vast influx of silver could not prevent the bankruptcy of the Spanish crown. It overextended itself in military adventures in Europe and all around the globe. The rulers ran up huge debts, mostly to foreign creditors, while the river of silver drove prices way up in a domestic economy already weakened by a drop in production of food and a rise in the importation of foreign manufactured goods. In the end, the conquest of ''the Indies'' led Spain to impoverishment and defeat.

But the accomplishments of the adventurous European sailors introduced the modern era. Their voyages connected Europe with the coasts of nearly the whole world. Remarkably, in not much more than one generation, every human society close by a shore was reached by ships sailing the world's new sea-lanes.

''Western Europe,'' wrote the historian William McNeill, ''of course was the principal gainer from this extraordinary revolution in world relationships, both materially and in a larger sense, for it now became the preeminent meeting place for novelties of every kind. This allowed Europeans to adopt whatever pleased them in the tool kits of other peoples and stimulated them to reconsider, recombine, and invent anew within their own enlarged cultural heritage.''

The losers were the Native Americans. In Mexico and Peru, their sophisticated cultures were crushed after their ruling classes were wiped out or demoralized by the invading Spaniards. Military force, disruption, uprooting, enslavement, and the famine and disease that accompanied them, destroyed the Native American cultures.

When the two cultures collided—that of the Europeans and that of the Indians—it ended with the Europeans dominant. They

*Sketches from Oviedo's manuscript
about the Indies, written in the
early 1500s, depicting Indian labor
forced to mine gold for the Spanish*

overwhelmed the Indians, who refused to be assimilated by the winners.

But the Indians exerted a strong cultural influence on their white conquerors. Peter Farb, one of the leading historians of the Native Americans, describes it:

> About half the states have Indian names, and so do thousands of cities, towns, rivers, lakes, and mountains. Americans drink hootch, meet in caucus, bury the hatchet, give clambakes, run the gauntlet, smoke the peace pipe, hold powwows, and enjoy Indian summer. The epithet ''skunk'' that the frontiersmen hurled so freely at the Indian is itself derived from an Indian word, as are many others in the English language. The march of settlers westward often followed the same trails that the Indians had used, and eventually these developed into today's network of concrete highways.
>
> Indians supplied the Europeans with foods that were new to them, taught them to plant and to hunt with Indian methods, guided them safely through a dangerous wilderness, and equipped them with tools and techniques that enabled them to survive. The plunder the Europeans were thus given the means to take, in gold and other treasures, built up the European nations and in part laid the groundwork for the industrial revolution.
>
> More than fifty new foods first domesticated by Indians were carried back to the Old World, including turkey, maize, white potato, pumpkin, squash, peppers, the so-called Jerusalem artichoke, tomato, avocado, chocolate, and several kinds of beans. The European has turned for relief to drugs and pharmaceuticals the Indians discovered: tobacco, quinine, ephidrine, novocaine, curare, ipecac, and witch hazel. Moccasin-style shoes are patterned after Indian footware; canoes, after their birchbark craft; toboggans, after their sleds; and

Indians fishing off the coast of North Carolina.
A watercolor by John White, ca. 1585.

apparel worn at ski resorts is copied from Eskimo clothing. We make use of other Indian inventions as well, including the snowshoe, hammock, poncho, parka, rubber ball, and even the syringe. The Constitution of the United States and those of several state governments were partly influenced by the democratic traditions of Indian societies.

What Farb refers to at the very end of this passage is the focus of a study made by another historian of Indian life, William Brandon. In his book *New Worlds for Old,* he proposes that from the reports of Columbus and Vespucci and the many other explorers who followed them, Europeans saw that the Indian societies of the New World were mostly built upon foundations radically different from those of the Old World. "The one greatest dividing difference," he says, "fell in the attitude toward property."

Peter Martyr, the Italian humanist who was the first historian of the New World, collected the fullest information possible on the newly discovered lands across the Atlantic. He interviewed the returned explorers, beginning with Columbus, on their observations of the Indians. And then he concluded, as Brandon puts it, that the Indians "lived a life free of toil and tyranny, free of master, free of greed and the struggle for gain." Among the people of the New World, wrote Martyr, "mine and thine (the seeds of all mischief) have no place." Land was held in common, free to all, "in open gardens, not divided with hedges or defended with walls. They deal truly with one another, without laws, without books, and without judges . . . in a free kind of life. Their ancient liberty makes them most happy of all men."

This basic equality, the living without masters, the liberty observed among the Indians by the explorers, became a new idea for Europeans. Brandon holds that it opened their eyes to an alternative way of life, to an ethic opposed to the belief in property and authority so fundamental to Old World attitudes.

Not that there was no cruelty and injustice, no misery and mayhem in Indian societies, he adds. But there was a different concept of liberty which took hold in Europe over the next few hundred years. It helped shape our present idea of liberty and equality for all.

A Note on Sources

My aim in this book is to tell the story of Columbus and to give the reader some idea of the Europe he sprang from and the America he came to. He stood astride two epochs: the Middle Ages and the Renaissance. How did that shape the man, his personality, his ideas, his ambitions? He made four voyages to the New World. What was that world like before his coming? How did the arrival of the white Europeans transform the world of the Native Americans? And, in turn, how did what the Europeans saw and did in the Americas change life in the Old World?

There are innumerable connections between the world of Columbus's time and the world we live in now. The impact of what he began is still felt, although 1992 marks 500 years since his arrival on these shores.

To develop this picture I have used a variety of sources, some of them discussed in the narrative. Mentioned there is the fact that only one log of Columbus's voyages—the first—survives, and not in full, original version. The most recent edition, translated and edited by Robert A. Fuson, is *The Log of Christopher Columbus* (International Maritime, 1988). Fuson sets the log in the framework of 15th century navigation and geography.

The Four Voyages of Christopher Columbus, edited by J. M. Cohen (Penguin, 1969) uses the log and excerpts from the writings of contemporaries of Columbus and his son Ferdinand. One of the earliest and most important accounts is *The History of the Indies,* by Bartolomé de Las Casas (Harper, 1971).

The best-known biography is *Admiral of the Ocean Sea: A Life of Columbus* (Northeastern, 1983) by Samuel Eliot Morison, Harvard professor and longtime student of his subject. Himself a sailor, Morison retraced in his own ship the voyages across the Atlantic. Although he does include the truth about the mass annihilation of the Indians, he gives it little weight in the balance against Columbus's navigational exploits.

To reach a wider audience Morison wrote a much shorter version called *Christopher Columbus: Mariner* (Signet, 1984). This book adds his translation of Columbus's own letter on his first voyage.

As a corrective to the viewpoint of Morison, there is Hans Koning's *Columbus: His Enterprise* (Monthly Review Press, 1976). His focus is on the fate of the Indians at the hands of the profit-driven discoverer and his men. An interesting psychological probing of the obsessive personality of Columbus is given by the Italian historian Gianni Granzotti in his *Christopher Columbus* (University of Oklahoma, 1987).

For background on the Europe of the time of Columbus, I used several books, among them: Marie Boas, *The Scientific Renaissance, 1450–1630* (Harper, 1963); J. H. Elliott, *The Old World and the New, 1492–1650* (Cambridge, 1970); J. R. Hale, *Renaissance Europe* (University of California, 1977); Robert M. Patten, editor, *Studies in Renaissance Science* (Noonday, 1961); and George Sarton, *The Life of Science* (Schuman, 1948).

Three marvelously detailed and highly stimulating studies of this era are contributed by J. H. Parry. *The Discovery of the Sea* deals with European and Asian maritime techniques, and *The Age of Reconnaissance* with political, economic, and religious factors in the overseas enterprise of 1450 to 1650 (both, University of California, 1981). And finally, Parry's *The Establishment of the European Hegemony, 1415–1715* (Harper, 1966) reviews trade and exploration in the age of the Renaissance.

I found Daniel Boorstin's *The Discoverers* (Vintage,1985) to be a superb story of what he calls "the heroic and imaginative thrusts of the great discoverers," including much, of course, on Columbus. Eric R. Wolf in his *Europe and the People Without History* (University of California, 1982) traces Europe's expansion and rise to world domination and the history of the common people who were both agents and victims in the historical process.

The case for the Jewish origins of Columbus is pursued in two books: Salvador de Madariaga's *Christopher Columbus* (Hollis & Carter, 1949) and Simon Wiesenthal's *Sails of Hope: The Secret Mission of Christopher Columbus* (Macmillan, 1973).

For the 400th anniversary of the discovery (1892) the Spanish government commissioned the German historian, Dr. Meyer Kayserling, to write *Christopher Columbus and the Participation of the Jews in the Spanish and Portuguese Discoveries*. The book demonstrates from rich archival sources the invaluable assistance provided to Columbus by many prominent Jews of his day. (First English edition, Carmi House Press, 1989).

On the people of the Americas who were here many thousands of years before Columbus arrived, there are many excellent studies. Some that I relied upon include William Brandon's *The Last Americans* (McGraw Hill, 1974) and his *New Worlds for Old* (Ohio University, 1986), which discusses how the Europeans entering the New World responded to the novel attitudes of the Indians toward property, authority, liberty, and the purpose of life. Peter Farb, in *Man's Rise to Civilization,* shows how much we have to learn about the creation of cultures anywhere in the world from the richly varied examples of the development of Indian civilization in the Americas. Jack D. Forbes, editor of *The Indians in America's Past* (Prentice Hall, 1964), uses varied sources to document the Native Americans' struggle against the invaders from Europe.

For almost all the books listed I have given the publisher and date of the paperback edition.

Index

Ceuta, 19, 20
Chanca, Diego, 124
China, 13, 16, 94, 158
Christianizing mission, 60,
    74, 92, 93, 112, 139–40,
    153, 171
Cibao, 102, 103
Colombia, 175
Colonial war, first in Amer-
    ica, 141
Columbus, Bartholomew
    (brother), 47, 61, 64, 113,
    139, 140, 154, 155, 161,
    162, 166, 168
Columbus, Christopher. *See
    also* Four Voyages, in-
    dexed separately: agree-
    ment with Spain, 67; ap-
    pearance, 41–42, 57; ar-
    rested, 155; arrogance,
    65, 69, 96, 101, 111;
    birth, 25, 37; books essen-
    tial to, 49; Catholic
    Church refuses beatifica-
    tion of, 175; as chart-
    maker, 47; conducts slave
    raids, 139–41; death,
    170; deposed as Indies
    governor, 158; as "discov-
    erer," 9; duplicity of, 84;
    early voyages, 42, 44, 47,
    52, 54; education, 27–28,
    41; fantasies, 110, 113;
    Genoa years of, 45–60;
    geographic misconcep-
    tions of, 175; greed for
    gold, 54, 74, 84, 112, 124,
    131, 165; illnesses, 159,
    163, 166, 169; income re-
    duced, 169; indifference
    to rape, murder, 131; in-
ept as administrator, 154;
    Jewish origins claimed,
    37; love affair, 61; made
    nobleman, 113; madness,
    154; marriage, 52; muti-
    lates Indians, 132; naviga-
    tional skills, 49, 54, 93,
    124, 147; parents, 38, 40;
    personal health, 159, 170;
    piety of, 54, 59, 103, 156;
    racist views, 88; secretive-
    ness, 72; shaping of leg-
    end about, 171; siblings,
    40; temperament, 57–59;
    terrorizes Indian rebels,
    140–41; as weaver, 41;
    willpower of, 72, 81
Columbus, Diego (brother),
    132, 154, 155
Columbus, Diego (son), 54,
    60, 75, 113, 139, 169
Columbus, Dominic (father),
    38, 40, 42
Columbus, Giovanni (grand-
    father), 38
Columbus, Susanna
    (mother), 38, 40
Copernicus, 35
Cordova, 61
Corn, 151
Cortés, Hernan, 175
Costa Rica, 163
Crusades, 12, 19, 54
Cuba, 94, 132, 135, 158,
    159, 161
Cuneo, Michele de, 124, 127

D'Ailly, Pierre, 16, 49
Diaz, Bernal, 19
Dias, Bartholomew, 60, 64,
    133, 148

Indians (*continued*)
110, 139, 141: Europeans view of, 88, 91; extermination of, 86, 144; feed marooned Spaniards, 167; first encounters with, 84–86; forced to pay tribute, 141–42; ignored in treaties, 117; kidnapped by Columbus, 99, 140; influence of upon Europeans, 178–81; massacred on Hispaniola, 159, 167; migrations of, 9; mutilated by Columbus, 132, 133, 142; origins of, 87; physical appearance, 89; population, 88, 144; raided for slaves, 139–41; raped by Spaniards, 127, 130, 140; refuse assimilation, 178; rise in revolt, 140–41; robbed by Spaniards, 142; views on property, 90, 180–81

Isabella (queen of Castile and Aragon), 61, 63–65, 75, 84, 99, 113, 117, 131, 144, 149–50, 154, 175

Italian traders, 12, 20

Jamaica, 132, 137, 147, 166, 168

Japan, 13, 60, 63, 77, 94, 102, 132

Jewish origins of Columbus, theory of, 37

Jews, expelled from Spain, 72, 74

John II (king of Portugal), 59–60, 64, 111, 115, 119

Labrador, 47, 156

La Cosa, Juan de, 69, 135, 148

Las Casas, Bartolomé de, 57, 75, 84, 96, 142, 174

Leonardo, 35–36

Lisbon, Columbus in, 41, 44, 45–54, 109, 111

Madariaga, Salvador de, 37

Madeira Islands, 22, 24, 52

Magellan, Ferdinand, 123

Maps: first inclusion of New World, 135; La Cosa's of 1500, 135, 148; pre-Columbian, 9; of Ptolemy, 15, 16, 20; spread by printing, 51, 52; Waldseemuller's of 1507, 172

Marchena, Antonio de, 61

Margarit, Mosén Pedro, 139, 140, 141

Margarita Island, 151

Martinique, 161

Martyr, Peter, 122, 148, 180

Mayans, 162–63

Medina Celi, Count, 61

Medina Sidonia, Duke, 61

Mediterranean trade, 20

Méndez, Diego, 167, 168

Mercator, Gerardus, 174

Mexico, 135, 175, 176

Middle Ages (medieval era), 25–36

Moors, Spain's war against, 63–64

Morison, Samuel Eliot, 123

Native Americans. *See* Indians

Natural History (Pliny), 49

DATE DUE

EAST WINDSOR JR/SR
HIGH SCHOOL